SANTA FE COOKERY

JIM DOUGLAS

SANTA FE COOKERY

Traditional New Mexican Recipes

The Dial Press
New York

Book Design by PLAZA GRAPHICS, Santa Fe, New Mexico.

Illustration copyright © 1982 by PLAZA GRAPHICS.

Photography by Brad Bealmear.

First printing.

Manufactured in the United States of America.

Library of Congress Cataloging in Publication Data

Douglas, Jim, 1931 -
    Santa Fe cookery.

Previously published as: The complete New Mexico cookbook. 1977.
    Includes index.
    1. Cookery, American — New Mexico. 2. Santa Fe (N.M.) — Social life and customs. I. Title.
TX 715.D688 1982 641.59789 82-5166 ISBN 0-385-27753-9 AACR2

Published in 1982 by The Dial Press
                1 Dag Hammarskjold Plaza
                New York, New York 10017

This book is dedicated to all the wonderful people and chefs of New Mexico, as well as to the following: Dave and Ida; Helen; John Nero; Bud and Addie; Claire; Allan; Binnie; Charlie Reid; Bill Burgess; Geoff; Dee; Fred and Georgina; R.B.; Bill Dorvillier; Mary; Marcos; Mick and Vic; Fred and Wanda; Rita and John; Alice; Barbara; Al; Abe; Gloria; Chago; Allene and Pete; Bob and the girls; Manuel and Jean; and Charlie Wasson.

TABLE OF CONTENTS

PREFACE

Santa Fe cookery has come into its own, and the word is spreading. One may think in terms of Southwest or Mexican—and there is a basis of fact in this—but there is indeed a definite difference, and you don't have to go any further than the New Mexico chili pepper for proof.

While the niceties and techniques of Santa Fe cookery have been practiced by residents and inquisitive visitors for centuries, sophisticated advances in farming, refrigeration, transportation, and merchandising have only recently made its exotic ingredients readily obtainable across the country, thereby encouraging millions more to delve into its glories.

No longer does the harried cook have to labor making tortillas from scratch, unless he or she wants to. And for the person-on-the-go, there are superb canned taco and enchilada sauces for immediate dispensing and dining.

Even New Mexico's famed chili is on supermarket shelves in neat cans, peeled and still whole; and both chopped red and green varieties can often be found in the frozen food department.

There's also a commercial tortilla flour, but you can buy ready-made tortillas in packages or cans. Even taco shells, ready for filling and heating, can be purchased far and wide today.

And as for sopaipillas—those delightful crusty fluffs of air that go so well with honey—well, there's also a mix if you don't care to take the time to stir up the flour, baking powder, salt, and sugar yourself.

If these items and other such New Mexican food delicacies as pinto beans, different varieties of chili powder, posole, and piñon nuts aren't available in a particular area, an appendix has been included listing outlets and specialty stores where they can be obtained.

This book, then, was written not only as an introduction to the entire scope of New Mexican cookery, but as a definitive reference guide for the serious student.

But even with the basic recipes in hand, you will discover that the variations are endless, and the final result of any dinner, buffet, or snack is completely up to the tastes and imagination of the individual preparing it.

Once the rudiments are mastered, a cook can create, as in other culinary pursuits, by sight, feel, and taste, and make adjustments as necessary. For instance, chili and sauces can be made as hot or mild as you want, and no recipe needs to be followed to the letter. Such items as sour cream chopped tomatoes, lettuce, and onion can be added, subtracted, or minimized at will to suit varying palates.

No effort was attempted in this compilation to adjust the recipes within these pages for high altitude cooking even though mountainous New Mexico ranges from almost 3,000 feet above sea level near the caverns at Carlsbad to more than 13,000 feet near Taos in the northern part of the Land of Enchantment.

A chapter on high altitude cooking is also included should the reader be required to make some adjustments in these or other recipes.

All a cook basically needs to lay out a spread of New Mexican food in a matter of minutes are some fresh, frozen, or canned chilies, a stack of tortillas, pot of pinto beans, ripe tomatoes, cans of hot and mild enchilada sauce or stock in the back of the refrigerator, olives, grated cheese, onion, garlic, bacon fat (lard or oil), and lettuce.

At sea level or 10,000 feet, east or west, north or south, you will have discovered the finest in eating—Santa Fe style.

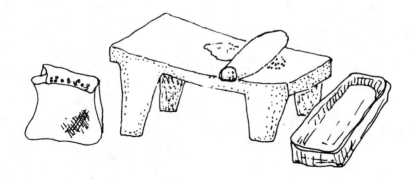

TORTILLAS

In the comic strip "B.C.," clams are humorously used as currency. If, however, the strip had been about the early settlers of Santa Fe, historically it would have been more appropriate, and just as funny, to have depicted the characters exchanging tortillas for goods and services.

Except for one fact: A lot of gold and silver was around in those days, and tortillas would hardly have stacked up to that which glittered. Tortillas probably would have been rated about a penny, and a pretty large one at that.

Money aside, the tortilla was and still is the "bread" of New Mexico. It can be eaten alone with or mostly without butter; it can be wrapped around meat, cheese and other fillings; in fact, it can be rolled, stacked, or cut up as one pleases according to the dish or recipe.

Basically tortillas are made of white cornmeal, but special flours and a blue cornmeal are available (see appendix on Outlets and Specialty Stores).

The Quaker Oats Co. of Chicago makes two tortilla mixes: Masa Harina, a combination of corn treated with lime water and specially ground corn flour, and Masa Trigo, composed of blended flour, shortening, salt, and leavening.

Both call for the addition of just water. One then only has to knead and roll the dough out into paper-thin, 6-inch circles and lightly brown the tortillas on a hot, lightly greased griddle. The exact recipe is printed on all Quaker packages.

There are, of course, ready-made tortillas on the market—white corn, blue corn, and flour—packaged, canned or frozen. Before using, though, they should be sprinkled with a little water to freshen them and then warmed in a 200-degree oven or under a low broiler flame.

By watering and heating them, it's easier to roll the tortillas for any particular purpose without their breaking. Ready-made taco shells are available, thus eliminating the fear of making that dish.

Tortillas are the basis for the favorites of Santa Fe cookery. "Soft" tortillas are used for tacos and enchiladas, while "hard" or toasted ones are used to make tostadas and corn chips. Flour tortillas, often larger and thicker than those made with cornmeal, are the basis for baked burritos.

BASIC TORTILLAS

3 cups white cornmeal
1½ teaspoons salt
½ cup shortening
1 cup lukewarm water

Combine the cornmeal with the salt and cut in half of the shortening. Work lightly with the fingers or pastry blender. Cut in the other half and gradually add just enough water so that the dough holds together (add more water if necessary). Knead the dough until smooth.

Divide into about 16 balls, the size of an egg or golf ball. Cover with a damp towel and let rest for 15 to 20 minutes.

Roll out each ball into a thin, 6-inch circle. Cook for 1 to 2 minutes on each side on an ungreased hot griddle until just lightly brown. Always serve hot (reheat if stored).

WHITE FLOUR TORTILLAS

4 cups all-purpose flour, sifted
2 teaspoons baking powder
2 teaspoons salt
¾ cup shortening
1½ cups lukewarm water or milk

Sift the flour with the baking powder and salt. Cut in the shortening with a pastry blender and then slowly add the water to make a pliable dough.

Make about 24 balls the size of medium eggs, cover with wax paper, and let stand for 15 to 20 minutes. Roll out into 6-inch circles on a floured surface and lightly brown on an ungreased hot griddle.

CHILI TORTILLAS
MAKES ABOUT 12

3 tablespoons chili
   powder
1 cup lukewarm water
2 cups Masa Harina
   powder
½ teaspoon salt

Add the chili powder to the water.
Mix with the Masa Harina and salt
until a smooth dough is formed.
Cover and let stand for 30 minutes.

Divide the dough into 16 balls and
roll out into 6-inch circles. Fry on
an ungreased griddle until dry and
lightly brown.

CORN CHIPS (Tostados)
MAKES 48

½ teaspoon chili powder
1 tablespoon salt
½ cup lukewarm water
12 white corn tortillas

Dissolve the chili powder and salt
in the water. Sprinkle both sides of
each tortilla and cut each into four
wedges. Let dry and then deep fry
until crisp.

Serve as potato chips or with
guacamole, refried beans, chili
con queso, or other appetizer tid-
bits.

4

PINTO BEANS

After you have had steak night after night—as the folk song goes—beans, beans are all right. In the case of the pinto bean, that's a gross understatement.

They're more than all right. They're a nutrient beyond compare, and supplemented with meat or cheese and chili or tomatoes constitute a perfectly-balanced diet. The flavor of the versatile pinto beans speaks for itself, whether used as a vegetable or in soups, salads, and sandwiches or as a meat substitute or even as the basis for a dessert.

Grown for centuries in large quantities in the semiarid climate of New Mexico—they were probably introduced by Spanish missionaries who transplanted them from Central America—the pinto is so-named because of its spotted appearance of dark, irregular splotches on a cream or buff background.

The pinto bean is an excellent low-cost source of energy, iron, and the important B complex vitamins. In addition, it is a source of protein and contains a significant amount of calcium. Small amounts of meat or cheese improve the quality of the protein, and chili or tomatoes provide vitamins A and C. Also, the presence of vitamin D in these beans makes them especially desirable in winter because during this time the diet is likely to be low in this much needed vitamin.

When preparing pinto beans, the first consideration is palatability. In order for pinto beans to have the best flavor, they should be cooked to the point when the skin is practically as tender as the inside of the bean. If they are to be served without mashing, the beans should not become broken or mushy.

In high altitudes, such as Santa Fe, the pinto bean requires a relatively long cooking period, but there are several methods by which the time may be shortened.

One of the simplest of these methods, and one which would apply anywhere, is the soaking process. The beans may be soaked overnight or until they have approximately doubled in size.

If the beans are cooked in soft water, they not only cook quicker but the flavor will be improved. If it's necessary to cook in hard water, it's advisable to boil the water first to remove the calcium salt, as it has been shown that calcium toughens the skin of the beans.

A pressure cooker will also materially shorten cooking time. Approximately 30 minutes at 15 pounds pressure will make the beans tender. Continued cooking for a few minutes in an open pot will remove the pressure cooker flavor that some people find objectionable.

Note: In Southest cookery, pinto beans are frequently referred to as "frijoles," but this is in error, as "frijol" is the Spanish word for bean and would indicate a bean of any variety.

SANTA FE PINTO BEANS

3 cups dried pinto beans
(2⅓ cups =
1 pound)
2½ quarts hot water
¼ pound salt pork or
cubed bacon
3 cloves garlic, peeled
1 teaspoon salt, or to
taste
1 teaspoon chili powder,
or to taste

Wash and pick over the beans, removing any loose skins or shriveled beans. Put in a large pot and cover with water. Soak overnight. Next day, wash the beans thoroughly in cold water, return to the pot, and add the hot water. Bring to a boil and simmer gently (do not boil violently) for about 3 hours, stirring occasionally. When the beans start to simmer, add the hunks of salt pork or the cubed bacon and the whole garlic cloves (they will be removed later). Add more hot or boiling water as needed. Never add cold water. The cooked juice should be thick. When the skins are almost as tender as the inside of the beans, they are done. They should not be broken. Add the salt and chili powder, stir, and allow to stand before tasting. Add more as desired.

SCALLOPED PINTO BEANS

2 cups dried pinto beans
¼ pound salt pork cut
into ⅛-inch cubes
2 medium onions, minced
4 tablespoons all-
purpose flour
1 teaspoon salt
Pepper to taste
2 cups water
½ cup bread crumbs

Cook the beans until they are tender. Place in a greased baking dish.

Brown the salt pork cubes in a skillet. Add the salt pork to the beans. Brown the onions in the salt pork fat and add to the beans. Mix the remaining fat with the flour, salt, and pepper. Stir in the water and add the mixture to the beans. Sprinkle the bread crumbs over the top and bake at 350 to 400 degrees for 20 minutes.

MASHED PINTO BEANS SERVES 8

2 cups dried pinto beans
6 cups hot water
2 tablespoons shortening
or butter
2 teaspoons salt

Soak the beans overnight. Drain and add the hot water. Cook the beans, making sure the liquid is thick and there is no surplus to make them watery. Mash with a spoon until the beans are broken up. Melt the shortening, add the beans and salt and cook for 15 minutes, stirring occasionally.

BAKED PINTO BEANS SERVES 12

4 cups dried pinto beans
¾ pound salt pork
2 tablespoons molasses
1½ tablespoons dry
mustard (optional)

Soak the beans overnight in cold water. In the morning, add fresh water and cook slowly until the skins begin to burst.

Turn the beans into a bean pot and bury the salt pork in the beans. Add the molasses and enough boiling water to cover the beans. Cover the pot and bake in a 300-degree oven for 6 to 8 hours. Add the dry mustard or 2 tablespoons prepared mustard, if desired.

REFRIED BEANS SERVES 8

2 cups drained, cold
cooked pinto beans
2 tablespoons bacon fat
or oil
4 tablespoons onion,
minced and sautéed
until tender
(optional)
4 tablespoons grated
Cheddar cheese
(optional)

Mash the cold cooked beans and fry in the hot bacon fat, stirring constantly until completely dry. Add the onion to the mashed beans. The grated cheese may be added as the beans cook slowly.

BUFFET PINTO BEANS

2 cups dried pinto beans
½ teaspoon salt
½ cup bacon fat
1 clove garlic, chopped
½ cup chopped onion
½ cup chopped green
   pepper
1½ teaspoons chili powder
½ teaspoon black pepper

Soak the beans overnight. Cover with fresh cold water and cook the beans until tender, adding more boiling water as necessary to end up with 2 cups of liquid. When the beans are tender, add the salt, stir well, taste and add more salt if desired.

Start to make a sauce by heating the bacon fat in a large skillet. Add the garlic, onion, and green pepper. Sauté until the onion is limp and transparent.

Scoop out 1 cup of the beans and drain off 2 cups of the liquid from the pot. Add ½ cup of the beans and 1 cup of the liquid to the skillet with the vegetables and mash thoroughly with a potato masher. Stir well, then add the remaining ½ cup of the beans and the other cup of liquid and mash again to make a sauce. Season with the chili powder and black pepper.

Cook this sauce until it is quite thick, stirring to prevent scorching or burning, and then stir into the beans, It will thicken while stirring, but since these beans should be quite thick, it will probably be necessary to let the beans simmer for a while to reach the proper consistency.

COWPUNCHER PINTO BEANS

SERVES 12

4 cups pinto beans
1 ham hock
2 small chilies
3 small onions, minced
2 tablespoons bacon fat
2 tablespoons chili powder
1 cup tomato juice

Soak the beans overnight. In the morning, put a small ham hock in a kettle with the beans and the water they soaked in. Add the 2 chilies and let simmer until the beans are tender.

Prepare a sauce by browning the onions in the bacon fat. Then add the chili powder and just enough water to steam the onions tender. Add the tomato juice and boil the mixture for 5 minutes. Remove the ham hock from the beans and take the meat from the bone, cutting it into small pieces. Return the meat to the beans and add the cooked sauce.

Let simmer for another ½ hour. These beans improve with each reheating.

HARD WATER COOKING

2 cups dried pinto beans
¼ teaspoon baking soda
5 cups water
2 teaspoons salt

Wash the beans. Dissolve the baking soda in the water, which has been heated to the boiling point. Soak the beans in the soda water for 10 to 14 hours. Boil gently in the same water until the beans are tender, for about 4 hours. Add the salt during the last half hour of cooking.

Helpful Hints: Boil the water for about 15 minutes before using for cooking or soaking. Use as small an amount of water as possible to keep the beans covered. Use a kettle with a tight-fitting lid to prevent evaporation. If beans are soaked, use hot water in soaking.

CHILI

In New Mexico cookery, the chili pepper is King. Long live the King! From as early as late July until frost, eager hands scoop up the freshly-picked, glossy green chili, peel them, chop them, stuff them, make sauces, can them, freeze them, and create the ultimate masterpiece—chili, a rather, all-encompassing term covering chili con carne and hundreds of variations.

Like religion, baseball, and politics, a debate on the virtues of making chili one way versus another is as senseless as trying to grow the tropical vegetable in snow.

Purists disdain any thought of putting tomatoes in chili. Others, however, like a mixture of ground beef, chopped chili or chili powder, onion, garlic, and tomatoes, while some prefer a simple, fiery soup of red or green chili, water, seasoning, and a little meat.

But no matter how used, whether in a chili sauce (salsa), taco and enchilada sauces, or chili rellenos, the New Mexico chili pepper (No. 6) is revered throughout the Southwest as the finest, and indeed it is often used for the most part as the basis for Texas chili, Arizona chili, or wherever the "best" chili is supposedly made.

11

Fanciers in New Mexico consume more chili per capita than any other state and more acreage is under cultivation than all other states combined.

The chili has a long history in New Mexico and its continuing development has led to its predominance in the field.

Although some historians say the Spaniards introduced the chili to New Mexico from tropical South America, where it dates back to 700 B.C., there is evidence that the Pueblo Indians were growing a mild version along the banks of the New Mexican stretch of the Rio Grande when the Spanish arrived in the 1500s.

Columbus found chili, the Aztec name for the plant, in the West Indies in 1493, and because of the pungency of the pods he called the plant pepper although it is not related to the shrub that produces black pepper.

It is classified as *Capsicum frutescens,* being in the nightshade family, which also includes tomatoes and potatoes. Chili's pungency comes from capsaicin, a bitter compound in the flesh and clear white seeds.

Columbus took some chili back home with him that year, and by 1548 it was growing in England and by 1585 in central Europe.

Though a perennial in its native habitat of tropical America, chili grows as an annual in temperate zones. It grows only under irrigation in New Mexico. Chili was grown successfully under irrigation in 1600, as were Spanish wheat and Indian corn, and was a welcome addition along with the pinto bean to an otherwise bland diet.

The early native chili was exceedingly variable and much of it was of poor grade. Efforts were initiated to develop a larger, smoother, thicker-meated, shoulderless pod of chili.

In 1907, Fabian Garcia, later director of what is now the New Mexico State University's Agricultural Experiment Station, started this search. From fourteen different strains, he broke them down to a single one, No. 9, by 1917.

This chili, which became famous as College No. 9, was adequate, but a need developed for other varieties of varying hotness. In fact, No. 9 was considered too hot to market on a large scale in the Midwest.

Then in 1955, New Mexico No. 6 was developed and put into production, and it proved to be a commercial success, being milder, in New Mexico as well as elsewhere.

The result was more or less a uniform pod 6 to 8 inches long and about 2 inches wide, smooth, fleshy with little waste, shoulderless at the stem end, and easy to peel. Commercial processors of green chili use more of this variety than any other.

Others in demand are Rio Grande-21, of medium pungency, also popular with commercial processors, and Sandia A, possessing the high pungency and flavor of the unimproved native chilies which date back to the sixteenth century and still grow in the northern valleys.

A new strain, Numex Big Jim, went into commercial production in 1974 and ranks between the Rio Grande and Sandia chilies on the hotness scale. A breakthrough was accomplished with the Numex Big Jim in that three of the foot-long pods generally weigh a pound, thus making machine-picking possible on larger tracts of irrigated land.

These varieties are used for fresh green chili in season, for canning, freezing, and drying commercially and for home processing.

Besides its renowned flavor and versatility, chili is a rich source of vitamins A and C and also serves as a preservative in frozen-stored cooked meat dishes.

Red chili retards the oxidation of fats and so delays rancidity and its consequent off-flavors. Chicken, beef, and pork casseroles have a longer frozen-storage life when they contain chili.

As the pods mature and ripen, the carotene (vitamin A) content increases, reaching its highest values in the ripe fresh peppers. Canned or frozen green or red chili retains most of the carotene content. Even after being dried, the red retains most of its carotene content.

The ascorbic acid (vitamin C) content of chili also increases as the season advances. Research has shown that green chili gathered in October contains more ascorbic acid than that picked in August. The highest values are often found in pods gathered just before they ripen.

Ascorbic acid, however, is more affected by heat and oxidation than vitamin A. Canned or frozen chili retains about two thirds of its ascorbic acid content. But red chili loses its vitamin C when dried, regardless of the method used.

Dry red chili is a staple item in markets throughout New Mexico. The dried pods are sold whole or ground into powders which are usually labeled as to their pungency. Shoppers almost always need to know whether the chili is mild or hot, regardless of its form—fresh, canned, frozen, or dried.

High-quality dry whole pods are an even red color. Pods should be free of black mold spots to avoid waste.

Fresh chili with good texture, flavor, and vitamin content will have a bright shiny surface and well-rounded smooth shoulders. They will be easy to peel and there will be little waste.

Avoid immature, shriveled, dull-looking or ill-shaped pods, as they are usually difficult to peel, may lack characteristic flavor and may be lower in vitamin content.

When possible, fresh chili, green and red, should be purchased in amounts that will be used within 3 days for best flavor, texture, vitamin values, and appearance. Freshly-gathered pods peel more easily than those kept for a few days. Also, crisp pods peel easier than wilted, limp ones. Store chili in polyethylene bags in the refrigerator until ready to use.

Frozen chili products should be stored at 0 degrees F., or lower. Frozen items should be protected from thawing from the market to home freezer. Texture, flavor, appearance, and nutrient content of chili are lowered when it is allowed to thaw and refrozen.

Canned chili should be stored in a cool, dark place before it's opened and should be refrigerated after opening. It should also be used within a day or two to avoid loss of flavor and vitamin content.

Dried red chili and chili powder should be kept in a cool, dark spot. Dried red chili, like any other spice or herb, loses flavor and appearance when stored at warm room temperatures.

Red chili is harvested before the first frost (September 16 to October 7) and dried by spreading them out on lath racks or netting, by laying them out on flat rooftops, or simply by drying them on the hard-baked adobe ground.

In the fall Santa Fe homes are aglow in the scarlet splendor of long and short ristras and wreaths of chili. Ristras are made by tying three or four chili together at the stems with short pieces of string which are then fastened in tiers of clusters, one atop the other, on a long, strong cord.

Ristras may run 5 feet long or more, and may be looped into a double strand. They are hung where the air circulates well and are picked and ground as needed.

Ristras and wreaths are available by mail (see appendix on Outlets and Specialty Stores) and make beautiful winter decorations.

The peeling of fresh green chili can be an aggravating, troublesome, and clumsy experience, but the resulting bowlfuls of delightful, chopped chili ready for immediate use, canning, or freezing are equally satisfying and tongue-tingling.

There is no single way to remove the tough transparent outer skin. However, there are several accepted practices that can make an easy job of the process. They are:

1. The oven or broiler method.
2. The direct heat method.
3. The hot paraffin dip method.
4. The oil dip method.

To do in the oven, slit one side of each chili pod or puncture several times with a fork. To lower pungency, remove seeds and veins before the pods are blistered. Place chili on a baking sheet or in a pan 3 to 5 inches below the broiler unit.

Use the high position on a electric range or medium flame on a gas stove. The broiler door should be left open and the pods turned frequently so that they will blister evenly and not burn.

They can also be prepared in a 450-degree oven and turned as above.

When the pods are blistered on all sides, they should be removed from the heat and either steamed in a wet towel for 15 minutes or plunged immediately into ice water.

Then, starting at the stem end, the skin is peeled downward. When the stem is broken off, most of the seeds should come off with it. The membrane is also removed.

Note: For those with tender skin, rubber gloves are advised for the handling of the chilies in the peeling process. Avoid touching the face either with or without gloves. In case of a burning sensation, wash with soap and water.

The pods can also be blistered on a wire mesh placed directly over a heating unit on top of the stove or done on an outdoor grill. As in the oven-broiler method, a medium flame is used on a gas stove and high on an electric one. The pods are again frequently turned to prevent burning. Then, they are either steamed or plunged into ice water and peeled starting with the little end, stripping to the stem and removing the seeds.

Some cooks prefer not to peel each chili after blistering unless they are to be used right away. They feel that peeling is easier and less time-consuming if the pods are frozen in small packages, then thawed and used as needed.

The stems and most of the seeds should be removed from the blistered pods before steaming and the chili placed in freezer containers. If the freezer is heavily loaded, place containers along with sides and bottom to attain 0 degrees F. and below.

Freezing the blistered, unpeeled pods reduces the preparation time for freezing. Also, fewer pods are broken. Apparently the thin skin, although blistered, serves as a shield and results in attractive pods for such uses as chili rellenos.

The third way to peel chili is the hot paraffin dip method. First, melt the paraffin over water. Wash the

17

chilies and dry each pod thoroughly to prevent the hot fat from spattering. Prick the skins with a needle or fork to prevent pods from exploding in the hot fat. It is best to keep the holes small.

Heat the paraffin over low direct heat to about 300 degrees. Don't get the oil too hot. Have a lid handy in case of flash fire. Put only 2 peppers in hot oil at one time. Use a wire basket or tongs.

Allow the chili to turn white or blister all over for 2 minutes. Plunge the blistered peppers into ice water immediately. Remove skin along with the paraffin by working on paper to make cleaning up easier.

Remove the stems and seeds with a knife. If desired, leave the chilies whole and press flat to remove air if for canning or freezing.

The final method is the hot oil dip. Again, wash, dry, and prick as for the hot paraffin dip. Heat cooking oil to 360 degrees. Put 2 peppers at a time in the hot oil and blanch for 2 to 3 minutes.

Plunge into ice water and wipe the oil off with paper. Slip off the skins and then remove the stems and seeds.

Some people object to the use of oil as it may adhere to the chili and make it hard to handle. It can also affect the flavor if rancid oil is used. When all of the oil has not been removed from canned chili, it will become rancid if stored in a warm place.

To freeze, chilies peeled by these hot processes need no further blanching. They should be packed in small moisture-vapor-proof containers or bags and filled to the shoulder of glass jars.

Containers suitable to the size of a family should be used and the chilies used soon after thawing. Packages should be placed in the coldest part of the freezer for fast freezing. Labels indicating product and date of freezing should be attached to each container.

Like tomatoes, green chilies must be canned under pressure to avoid the danger of botulism. Fresh green and red chilies can and freeze well.

To can in a pressure canner, select fresh, tender chilies and wash carefully. Remove the skins, stems, and seeds by your favorite method. Pack the prepared chilies loosely in jars to within 1 inch of the top.

Cover with boiling water to insure a more even temperature. Add salt, ¼ teaspoon for each half pint, if desired, and adjust the lids of the jars.

Place the hot containers on the rack in the canner. Fasten the lid on tight so that no steam escapes around the edge. Let the steam escape from the petcock for a full 10 minutes. Then close petcock.

As soon as the gauge registers the correct pounds pressure for any given altitude, control the heat unit to keep an even pressure for the time recommended for processing (see table below).

At the end of the processing period, turn off the heat or slide to cooler spot on the stove and let cool normally. It will take 20 to 25 minutes for the gauge to return to zero.

As soon as the gauge returns to zero, open the petcock slowly and wait for 5 minutes before opening the lid on the cooker. To remove the lid on the cooker, tilt far side up to protect the face.

Arrange the jars to cool quickly out of a draft and uncovered. The next day, check the seals on the jars. Label, polish, and store them in a cool, dark, dry location.

Minutes to Process		Pounds Pressure for Altitudes of:			
Jars		2-4,000	4-6,000	6-8,000	8-10,000
½ pint: 30	1 pint: 35	12	13	14	15

To can in a pressure saucepan, select, prepare, and pack the chilies as for a pressure canner. But then put 1 quart of hot water in pressure saucepan if 4 pint jars are to be processed, or 1½ quarts if half pints are to be used.

Fasten the lid in place on pressure saucepan as directed. Bring up pressure and regulate the heat to hold at 15 pounds pressure. Start counting process time after the pressure is up, 30 minutes for half pints and 35 for pints.

At the end of the process time, turn off the heat. For cooling, let the pan stand unopened, 20 minutes for half pints and 25 for pints. This is an essential part of the process when using a pressure saucepan.

At the end of the cooling time, open the exhaust to release any remaining steam before opening the lid on the pan. Remove the jars and cool away from a draft.

The next day, check the seals, label, and store in a cool, dark, dry spot.

All of the following recipes for chili, as well as those for sauces, dips, and vegetables, can be adjusted to suit individual tastes. Experience and conditioning will dictate whether to use mild, medium, or hot chili and chili powder and how much to use.

CHILI CON CARNE (Meat)

8 pounds lean beef, cubed
4 tablespoons lard
4 large onions, chopped
½ cup all-purpose flour (optional)
4 cloves garlic, minced
1 teaspoon dried oregano
½ teaspoon ground cumin
4 cups chopped green chili
6 cups hot water
Salt to taste

Brown the meat in the lard (lard produces the most authentic flavor). Add the onions and fry along with the meat until tender. Stir the flour into the meat-onion mixture. (If a thinner chili is desired, do not add the flour.) Add the garlic, oregano, cumin, and chili. Stir in the hot water and simmer for several hours. Season with salt to taste.

Note: Other meats, alone or combined, such as pork, mutton, deer, moose, elk, and goat, may be used instead of the beef.

(Tomatoes)
CHILI CON CARNE

1 pound lean ground beef
½ cup chopped onion
2 tablespoons cooking oil or lard
1 tablespoon all-purpose flour
1 (1-pound) can tomatoes with liquid
2 cloves garlic, minced
1 cup chopped green chilies, or 3 tablespoons chili powder
½ teaspoon dried oregano
¼ teaspoon ground cumin
Salt to taste
1 cup or more hot water

Brown the meat and the onions in the oil. Stir in the flour. Mash the tomatoes and add along with the liquid. Add the garlic, chilies, oregano, and cumin. Season with salt to taste. Add the water, bring to a boil, and simmer, covered, for 2 to 3 hours.

CHILI CON
CARNE WITH BEANS *SERVES 12*

1 cup dried pinto beans
4 cups water
2 tablespoons fat or cooking oil
½ cup chopped onion
2 pounds lean ground beef
2 (1-pound) cans tomatoes with liquid
2 tablespoons chili powder
All-purpose flour (optional)

Soak the pinto beans overnight. Then cook them in the 4 cups water until tender. Melt the fat in a large skillet and brown the onion. Add the ground beef and cook until it has lost its red color. Add the beans and mashed tomatoes with their liquid. Stir in the chili powder and bring to a boil. Reduce heat, cover, and cook until the meat is tender and the flavors well blended. The mixture may be thickened with a little flour if it is too thin.

Note: Avoid a greasy and over-seasoned dish. Use lean round, rump, flank, or chuck.

(Chicken)
CHILI CON POLLO *SERVES 4*

1 2½- to 3-pound broiler chicken
3 cups water
1 clove garlic, chopped
Salt
1 medium onion, minced
1 cup uncooked rice
2 tablespoons bacon fat
1 cup green chili sauce (see p. 59)
Pepper to taste

Cut the chicken into serving pieces. Simmer in the water with the garlic and 1 teaspoon salt for 1 hour, or until tender.

Sauté the rice and the onions in the fat until they are lightly browned. Add the green chili sauce and bring to a boil. Remove the cooked chicken from the pot and set aside. Add 2 cups of the chicken cooking liquid to the rice mixture and simmer until the rice is dry and fluffy. Add the cooked chicken to the rice and heat to blend all flavors. Season with salt and pepper to taste.

CHILI AND CHEESE CASSEROLE

4 tablespoons butter
1 cup cracker crumbs
12 large green chilies
1 pound grated Cheddar
  cheese
4 eggs
1 teaspoon salt
2 cups milk

Melt the butter in a small skillet and add the cracker crumbs. Cook, tossing and stirring, until the crumbs are lightly browned.

Peel the chilies, removing the stems and seeds. Chop the chilies. Place alternate layers of the chilies and cheese in a greased 13x9x2-inch baking dish. Reserve enough cheese to sprinkle on top. Beat the eggs slightly, then add the milk and salt. Pour over the chilies and cheese. Sprinkle the remaining cheese and the buttered cracker crumbs on top. Bake for 45 minutes in a 325-degree oven.

ENCHILADAS

If chili is King, then enchiladas reign as Queen in Santa Fe cookery.

Literally translated from the Spanish, enchilada means "chilied up," and truly it is a marriage of the chili to the tortilla with a wedding party of many ingredients for an ever-to-be-remembered feast.

The tortilla is the basis of the enchilada. It is usually rolled around meat, chicken, cheese, or other filling and baked in a hot chili sauce. But the tortillas can also be stacked, folded, or layered, baked or put under a broiler, and even fried and covered in a rich, red enchilada sauce.

Imagination rules in this gala procession, starting with the white or blue corn tortilla, adding or not chopped onion to the filling and topping off with grated cheese, sliced avocados, or sour cream as desired.

It must be remembered that the tortillas used for enchiladas are not toasted as they are for tostadas. If already made, they should be sprinkled with water to freshen them and then fried quickly in hot oil only until they are soft. Keep warm until ready to use.

STACKED ENCHILADAS *SERVES 4*

1 10-ounce can enchilada sauce or 1 10-ounce can home-made chili sauce (see p. 59)
12 white or blue corn tortillas (see p. 3)
4 tablespoons shortening
½ pound Cheddar cheese, grated
2 medium onions, chopped

Heat the enchilada or chili sauce in a small skillet until it is steaming.

In another skillet, fry the tortillas one at a time in the hot shortening for a few seconds until soft. Drain the tortillas and then immerse them in the hot sauce. Place one on each of four oven-proof plates and sprinkle with some grated cheese and chopped onion. Pour over some sauce. Repeat twice more, making a stack of 3 tortillas on each plate. Pour the remaining sauce over the stacks and top with more cheese.

Bake for 10 minutes at 350 degrees, or put under the broiler until the cheese melts. If desired, a fried-over-easy egg may be served on top of each enchilada stack, or chopped tomatoes and lettuce may be used as a garnish.

ROLLED ENCHILADAS *SERVES 4*

12 corn tortillas (see p. 3)
4 tablespoons shortening
2 medium onions, chopped
½ pound Cheddar cheese, grated
1 10-ounce can enchilada sauce or homemade chili sauce (see p. 59)

Fry the tortillas one at a time in the hot shortening. Drain.

Fill each tortilla with some chopped onion and grated cheese and roll tightly. Place side by side in a shallow 13x9x2-inch baking dish. Cover with the enchilada or chili sauce and top with more grated cheese.

Heat at 350 degrees, or put under the broiler until hot and the cheese is melted.

MEAT FILLING

1 onion, chopped
1 clove garlic, minced
1 tablespoon cooking oil
1 pound ground chuck
Salt to taste
½ cup grated Cheddar
   cheese
1½ cups enchilada sauce
   (see pp. 62-63)
12 corn tortillas (see p. 3)

Sauté the onion and garlic in the oil until soft, add the meat and brown. Season with salt to taste. Add the cheese and enchilada sauce and heat thoroughly. Fry and dip 12 corn tortillas as in the recipe for Rolled Enchiladas. Put the filling across and roll tightly. Continue as for Rolled Enchiladas.

CHICKEN FILLING

3 cups shredded cooked
   chicken
½ cup slivered almonds
½ cup grated Cheddar
   cheese
1½ cups enchilada sauce
   (see pp. 62-63)

Mix and heat all ingredients. Lay the filling across 12 corn tortillas prepared as for Rolled Enchiladas and continue as above. Serve topped with sour cream and chopped green onion, if desired.

CHEESE FILLING

3 cups grated Cheddar
   cheese
6 green onions, sliced
1½ cups enchilada sauce
   (see pp. 62-63)

Mix and heat all ingredients. Divide the filling and place 12 corn tortillas prepared as for Rolled Enchiladas. Proceed as above.

ENCHILADA CASSEROLE *SERVES 6 TO 8*

2 pounds lean ground
    beef
  Cooking oil or fat
2 cups chopped green
    chilies
2 cups water
1 teaspoon salt
24 corn tortillas (see
    p. 3)
1 cup chopped onion
2 cups grated Cheddar
    cheese
1 large tomato, thinly
    sliced
1 cup chopped lettuce

Brown the meat in a little oil. Add the green chilies and water. Season with the salt and simmer for 5 minutes, or until the sauce thickens. Dip the tortillas in some hot oil and fry until crisp but not hard on both sides. Then cover the bottom of an oiled 13x9x2-inch casserole by overlapping 6 of the tortillas. Spread half of the onion, cheese, and meat chili mixture over the tortillas. Repeat starting with the remaining tortillas and ending up with the cheese. Bake at 350 degrees until the cheese melts. Arrange the tomato slices on top and garnish with the chopped lettuce. Cut into squares

PORK ENCHILADAS *SERVES 6*

2 cups cooked pork,
    cubed
1 cup grated Cheddar
    cheese
1 medium onion, chopped
1 can condensed cream
    of mushroom soup
1 can condensed
    tomato soup
1 cup chopped green
    chilies
1 10-ounce can
    enchilada sauce
12 corn tortillas
½ cup sliced black
    olives
  Chopped lettuce and
    tomatoes

Combine the pork, half of the grated cheese, and the onion.

In a saucepan, mix the soups, chilies, and enchilada sauce and heat to boiling.

Fry the tortillas until pliable and then dip into the chili enchilada sauce.

Divide pork mixture among the tortillas, roll up and place in a 13x9x2-inch baking dish. Pour the remaining sauce over and sprinkle with the rest of the grated cheese. Bake at 350 degrees for 25 to 30 minutes. Garnish with olives, lettuce, and tomatoes.

CHORIZO ENCHILADAS

1 pound chorizo sausage
1 pound ground beef
2 medium onions, chopped
2 tablespoons cooking oil
1 cup chopped green chilies
2 10-ounce cans enchilada sauce
2 teaspoons salt
24 corn tortillas (see p. 3)
2 cups grated Cheddar cheese
  Chopped lettuce and tomato

Sauté the chorizo, beef, and onions in the hot oil until brown. Add the chilies, enchilada sauce, and salt. Simmer for 5 minutes.

Prepare in stacked fashion, alternating a tortilla, chorizo chili sauce mixture and grated cheese, three to a plate. Bake at 350 degrees for 10 minutes and garnish with chopped lettuce and tomato.

SERVES 8 # GREEN CHILI ENCHILADAS

1 can condensed cream of mushroom soup
1 can condensed cream of chicken soup
1 cup sour cream
1 cup milk
2 cups chopped green chilies
1 cup diced cooked chicken
1 medium onion, chopped
1 teaspoon salt
24 corn tortillas (see p. 3)
2 cups grated Cheddar cheese
1 head lettuce, chopped
4 large tomatoes, cut in wedges

Combine the mushroom and chicken soups, sour cream, milk, chilies, chicken, onion, and salt.

Mix well and bring just to a boil. Serve either in stacks, rolled, or layered in a casserole, alternating tortillas, chicken mixture and grated cheese. Garnish with chopped lettuce and tomato wedges.

VEGETARIAN ENCHILADAS *SERVES 4*

1 onion, chopped
2 cloves garlic, minced
½ pound mushrooms, sliced
1 green pepper, chopped
2 tablespoons cooking oil
1 1-pound can tomatoes with liquid
1 cup cooked drained pinto beans
1 tablespoon chili powder
½ teaspoon dried oregano
½ teaspoon dried thyme
¼ teaspoon ground cumin
Salt to taste
12 corn tortillas (see p. 3) fried until crisp
1½ cups grated Cheddar cheese

Sauté the onion, garlic, mushrooms, and pepper in the hot cooking oil. Add all the other ingredients except the tortillas and grated cheese. Simmer for 1 hour, adding a little hot water if necessary.

Put a layer of tortillas in a greased casserole. Spread a layer of sauce over them and then some grated cheese. Repeat until all the ingredients are used, topping off with cheese.

Bake at 350 degrees for 15 to 20 minutes. Cut into squares. This can also be made in stacked fashion, using 2 to 3 tortillas per serving, either baked in the oven or put under the broiler until the cheese is melted and garnished with chopped lettuce and tomatoes. Olives make a nice garnish for this dish.

TACOS

Tacos are to Santa Fe cookery what pretzels are to beer. One can just keep on eating finely fried, crisp tortillas wrapped around a savory filling and doused with a mild to hot chili sauce, or so it seems. And beer is not a bad accompaniment either.

The combination plate aside, after you have had an order of tacos, you've had it all. Well, almost.

As mentioned before, ready-made taco shells are available in some markets outside New Mexico, all stores in-state. But they are easy enough to prepare, starting with either homemade or store-bought tortillas.

The tortillas are fried one at a time in about ½ inch of hot oil. After a few seconds, they are turned, folded in half, and cooked to the desired crispness.

They are then drained and kept warm in a low-heat oven. To serve, the folded tortillas are opened gently and a filling of beef, pork, chicken, turkey, cheese, or pinto beans is carefully inserted.

Again, imagination, likes, or dislikes dictate what else goes in the taco, which can be either fried or baked for added crispness. Some of the usual condiments include chopped lettuce, tomato, onion, grated cheese, guacamole, and sour cream.

Mini tacos make excellent appetizers, as do many of the other main dishes within this book which can be adapted to fit the occasion.

BEEF TACOS

1 pound ground beef
1 medium onion, chopped
1 clove garlic, minced
2 tablespoons cooking oil
1 8-ounce can tomato
   sauce
   Salt and pepper
12 taco shells
   Chopped lettuce
   Chopped tomatoes
   Grated Cheddar
   cheese
1 8-ounce can green
   chili sauce or taco
   sauce (see pp. 59-61)

Sauté the beef, onion, and garlic in the hot cooking oil until brown. Add the tomato sauce and simmer for a few minutes. Season with salt and pepper to taste.

Warm the taco shells at 350 degrees for 5 minutes. Then place a heaping tablespoon of meat mixture in each shell and stuff with lettuce, tomato, and cheese as desired. Serve with the chili sauce or taco sauce. Top with sour cream or guacamole for an extra taste treat.

CHICKEN TACOS

¼ cup chopped green
   onion
1 tablespoon shortening
2 cups shredded cooked
   chicken
1 cup chopped green
   chilies
1 8-ounce can taco
   sauce
   Salt to taste
12 taco shells
1 cup grated Cheddar
   cheese
   Chopped lettuce
   Chopped tomatoes
   Sour cream
   Guacamole

Sauté the onion in the shortening until transparent. Add the chicken, green chilies, ½ can taco sauce, and salt to taste. Heat to boiling.

Warm the tortilla shells. Put 2 tablespoons of the chicken mixture and 1 tablespoon of grated cheese in each shell. Serve with lettuce, tomato, sour cream or guacamole and extra taco sauce, as desired.

TURKEY TACOS

SERVES 4

1 onion, chopped
1 tablespoon cooking oil
2 cups cubed cooked
   turkey
1 1-pound can tomatoes,
   drained
1 cup chopped green
   chilies
½ cup chopped walnuts
  Salt
12 tortilla shells
   Lettuce leaves
   Avocado slices

Sauté the onion in the hot oil until tender. Add the turkey, tomatoes, chilies, walnuts, and salt to taste. Simmer about 5 minutes.

Prepare the tortilla shells. Put some filling in each and fry in hot oil or bake at 350 degrees for 5 to 10 minutes.

Serve on the lettuce leaves and top with slices of ripe avocado.

CHEESE AND GREEN CHILI TACOS

SERVES 4

3 cups grated Cheddar
   cheese
1 cup chopped green
   chilies
  Salt
12 taco shells
   Cooking oil

Put ¼ cup of the cheese and about 1 tablespoon of the chilies in each taco shell. Sprinkle with salt. Roll and seal the shells with toothpicks and fry the tacos on both sides in the hot oil until crisp. Drain on paper towels before serving.

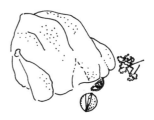

PINTO BEAN TACOS

2 cups cooked pinto beans
1 cup chopped green chilies
2 cloves garlic, minced
1 teaspoon salt
12 taco shells
2 tomatoes, chopped
1 onion, chopped
1 head lettuce, chopped
1 cup grated Cheddar cheese
1 8-ounce can taco sauce or chili sauce

Mash the pinto beans with the chilies, garlic, and salt. Put about 2 tablespoons of this mixture in each taco shell and place upright in a shallow baking dish. Fill with the chopped tomatoes, onions, and lettuce. Top each with some grated cheese. Bake at 350 degrees until the cheese melts. Serve with taco sauce or chili sauce.

TAMALES

Tamales are a traditional Christmas dish in Santa Fe cookery, but it's always a fiesta when they are put on the table.

Perhaps one of the reasons that they are served mainly on festive occasions is that they are time-consuming to prepare. It is best to make several dozen at a time and freeze some for later use.

Tamales may be made from scratch with *masa* or *nixtamalina,* a special fine-grade Mexican cornmeal. There are, however, other commercial meals available, the most popular being Masa Harina.

The masa dough is spread on cornhusks and filled with a variety of meats, then rolled, tied and steamed.

Tamale-making is one of the oldest pursuits of the Southwest Indians and naturally is one of the great delights of Santa Fe cookery.

The whole experience, however, is pretty well laid out by Bolner's Fiesta Products, Inc., of San Antonio, Texas. With their kind permission, here is the procedure from start to finish:

BOLNER
TAMALE EXPERIENCE   *MAKES 25 DOZEN*

3 pounds coarse ground beef
6 pounds coarse ground pork
10 ounces fresh chili pods
4 ounces fresh garlic
3 ounces ground cumin
Salt
2½ pounds cornhusks
12 pounds wet masa (fresh ground corn can be purchased). With dry masa, 10 pounds should be added with some water according to package directions
4 pounds (8 cups) pure lard
3 ounces chili powder
3 ounces paprika
3½ ounces garlic powder
2 12-quart cooking pots or tamale cans with lids

The day before:
Cook beef and pork in a low oven for 4 hours. When tender, remove meat and save the drippings.

Meanwhile, stem and seed the chili pods. If you pull off the stem and tear open the pods down one side while rinsing under running water, the seeds will fall out easily.

Simmer the pods in a covered pot of water for about 45 minutes, then remove from the heat and let cool. They should be a bright red color. Scrape the pulp from the skin, chop the pulp, and set it aside.

Also save the water gravy, but discard the skins as they tend to be bitter. Peel and chop the garlic and sauté in a couple of teaspoons of lard.

Combine and mix well the meat, sautéed garlic, chili pulp, 4 tablespoons cumin, and 4 table-spoons salt. Refrigerate overnight to allow all the spices to complete-ly permeate the meat for better taste.

The next morning:
Remove the meat from the refrigerator and warm to room temperature. Put all the cornhusks in a sink or tub and fill with warm water. They are inclined to float so you will have to weight (push) them down into the water. Soak for a minimum of 2 hours—the longer, the better.

The masa:
In a large bowl, place the 12 pounds wet masa. Gradually add

36

6 cups melted pure lard, sprinkle with 2 tablespoons chili powder, 8 tablespoons paprika, about 6 tablespoons salt, 2 cups chili pod gravy, 2 tablespoons garlic powder, and half of the meat drippings you saved from the cooked meat.

Work the mixture with your hands until thoroughly combined. Test the masa by dropping a small piece in a glass of water. If it doesn't float, add a little more melted lard, remix and test again. The main idea here is to work air into the masa until it is greasy and fluffy.

Begin separating the cornhusks one by one until you have a large stack ready.

Put about 2 inches of the broken shucks in the bottom of a large cooking pot or can and soak with water. This will keep the tamales from sticking and help to generate steam when it comes time to cook them.

The spreading:
Assemble some helpers (it is suggested that you have 4 or 5 people assisting) around the kitchen table. Everyone should have a flat plate or small tray and a butter knife or spatula.

Take an unbroken cornhusk and place it on the tray in front of you, the small end up, the opening toward you. Using the knife or spatula, dip into the bowl of masa and take out approximately 1 heaping tablespoon of masa.

Spread it on the shuck in such a way that it covers the lower two thirds of the right 4 inches of the shuck. The masa should be thick enough so that you cannot see through the shuck.

37

Next, spread some filling on the middle of the masa. The thickness of the masa and filling is strictly a personal preference. You decide how much masa you like around your filling.

The wrapping and steaming:
The tamale is then rolled over, starting from the side with the masa and the meat. The unspread side covers the outside and holds it together. The unfilled end is then folded over to the middle.

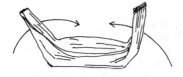

As you roll up the tamale, stand them shoulder to shoulder, open end up, around the bottom of the pot with the shucks in it.

After filling the pot, add water and put a lid on it. Steam for about 2 hours, or until the masa peels away from the shuck. You may have to occasionally add water in order to keep the pot from boiling dry.

Be sure to let the tamales cook for 10 to 15 minutes so they become firm before eating.

Note: All the dry ingredients in the above recipe may be obtained by mail from Bolner's Fiesta Products Co. See appendix on Outlets and Specialty Stores.

FRESH WHITE CORN MASA

MAKES 4 TO 5 DOZEN

3 dozen milky kernel corn on the cobs
1 tablespoon salt

Cut the kernels from the cobs and grind. Mix well with the salt. Use about 2 tablespoons per cornhusk following the directions for Tamales.

CHILI CON CARNE TAMALES

4 pounds lean stewing beef or pork
2 teaspoons salt
6 cups water
4 tablespoons chili powder
2 teaspoons chili pequin
1 tablespoon chili caribe
½ teaspoon dried oregano
2 cloves garlic, minced
6 cups Masa Harina
1 pound cornhusks

Simmer the meat and salt in the water until very tender. Remove the meat and shred it. Reserve the stock. Dissolve the three varieties of chili in 2 cups of the reserved stock and add to the meat along with the oregano and garlic. Cook until the liquid is almost absorbed.

Prepare the 6 cups Masa Harina as directed on the package, using the rest of the reserved meat stock.

Wash and trim cornhusks at both ends. They should be about 4 inches wide and 7 inches long. Soak in warm water at least 1 hour or until soft and pliable. When ready, shake water off the husks.

Spread about 2 tablespoons of the dough ¼ inch thick and 4 inches square in the middle of each husk. Put a heaping tablespoon of filling in the center of the dough. Fold over to seal in the filling, starting with the sides of the husk toward the center. Then fold up the bottom and close with the top. Tie with string or strands of discarded husk.

Stack the tamales loosely on a rack in a large steamer or covered roasting pan. Steam over boiling water for at least 1 hour, or until the tamales loosen off the husk. To test, remove one gently using a mitt or tongs. If the dough comes cleanly away, the tamales are done. These are good with either a red chili or mole sauce.

PINTO BEAN TAMALES   *SERVES 10 TO 12*

8 cups cooked drained
    pinto beans
2 tablespoons chili
    powder
2 cloves garlic, minced
2 teaspoons salt
3 dozen cornhusks,
    soaked
1 quart tomato sauce

Mash the pinto beans and mix with the chili powder, garlic, and salt. Shape into small rolls and wrap in the soaked cornhusks. Tie and simmer in a covered pan for 1 hour. Serve with your favorite hot sauce.

TAMALE PIE   *SERVES 8 TO 10*

1 pound lean ground
    beef
1 pound ground
    pork
1 large onion, chopped
2 cloves garlic, minced
¼ cup cooking oil or
    bacon fat
2 teaspoons salt
1 1-pound can tomatoes
    with liquid
½ cup sliced mushrooms
1 cup chopped green
    chilies or 2 table-
    spoons chili powder
1 cup cornmeal
1 cup water
3 cups boiling water
1 can ripe olives, sliced
½ pound Cheddar or
    Monterey Jack
    cheese, grated

Sauté the meats, onion, and garlic in the cooking oil until the meat is brown. Drain off the fat. Add 1 teaspoon of salt, or to taste. Add the tomatoes, mashed, and simmer for 1 hour, adding water if necessary. After 30 minutes, add the mushrooms and chili.

Mix the cornmeal with 1 cup water and the remaining salt. Then mix in the 3 cups boiling water. Cool.

Line a 13x9x2-inch casserole with half of the mush. Pour the meat mixture over the mush and spread evenly. Dot with the sliced olives and sprinkle the grated cheese over the top. Spread the remaining mush over the cheese. Bake at 350 degrees for about 45 minutes.

TOSTADAS

Tostadas are a bit different from enchiladas in that they are almost a meal by themselves, incorporating the bread, beans, meat, and salad in one dish.

Tostadas are crisp-fried tortillas served open-faced or stacked. Refried pinto beans are first spread over the tortilla, and then a meat or chicken mixture, lettuce, tomato, onion, and grated cheese, and even more tortillas, are piled as high as the appetite desires.

By their crisp nature, tostadas are also excellent for use as appetizers, cut into triangles and presented as canapés with refried beans, cheese, meat, guacamole, chili con queso, or even caviar.

The tostadas should be prepared shortly prior to serving as their crispness is lost should they stand too long.

TOSTADAS (Meat)
SERVES 4

1 pound lean ground beef
1 medium onion, chopped
1 clove garlic, minced
Cooking oil
1 8-ounce can tomatoes, mashed
½ cup chopped green chilies
1 teaspoon salt
¼ teaspoon dried oregano
8 corn tortillas
2 cups refried pinto beans
½ head lettuce, chopped
2 tomatoes, chopped
1 cup grated Cheddar cheese
Avocado slices
Pimiento-stuffed olives

Brown the meat, onion, and garlic in a little hot oil. Add the tomatoes, chilies, salt, and oregano. Simmer for 30 minutes, stirring occasionally.

Fry the tortillas on both sides until crisp. Drain on paper towels.

Place a tortilla on each plate and spread with some refried beans and then a layer of the meat mixture. Place another tortilla on top of the meat mixture and repeat layers. Cover with chopped lettuce and tomato. Garnish with grated cheese, avocado slices, olives, or sour cream, as desired.

CHALUPAS (Tostada boats)
SERVES 6

1 pound ground beef
½ onion, chopped
1 clove garlic, minced
Oil for frying
1 8-ounce can tomato sauce
1 cup chopped green chilies
12 corn tortillas
2 cups cooked pinto beans
1 cup grated Cheddar cheese
Chopped lettuce
Chopped tomatoes

Sauté the meat, onion, and garlic in 2 tablespoons hot cooking oil until brown. Add the tomato sauce and chilies and simmer until well blended.

Cut four 2-inch slits around each tortilla, about half way from the center to the edge. Fry the tortillas in about 1 inch of hot oil, holding down the centers so that the sides rise up to form a cup. Fry until crisp and then drain.

Divide the pinto beans and put into the cups. Divide the meat mixture and place on the beans. Top with the cheese and garnish with the lettuce and tomatoes.

CHORIZO-PORK TOSTADAS

1 pound chorizo sausage
1 pound pork, cubed
2 tablespoons bacon fat or lard
2 cups refried pinto beans
  Salt and pepper
12 corn tortillas
½ head lettuce, chopped
12 tablespoons olive oil
4 tablespoons wine vinegar
2 red chili pods, minced
½ cup grated Cheddar cheese

Brown the chorizo, which has been removed from its casing, and cubed pork in the lard or bacon fat. Add the refried beans and heat. Season with salt to taste.

Fry the tortillas until crisp.

Spread some of the sausage-pork mixture and beans over a tortilla placed on each plate. Mix the lettuce with the oil, vinegar, and minced chili pods. Season with salt and pepper. Put a layer of this on top of the sausage-pork mixture and beans, Repeat two more times. Sprinkle with the cheese. Bake at 350 degrees for 10 minutes, or until the cheese is melted.

EMPANADAS

Empanadas are another traditional Christmas dish, but they are always good as a snack at a cocktail party and a delightful way to use leftover meat, fish, or vegetables.

The turnovers can be filled, as suits the occasion, with mincemeat, fruit, shrimp, or spinach, as well as the more conventional meat or chicken.

MINCEMEAT EMPANADAS   *MAKES 12*

2 cups all-purpose flour,
    sifted
2 teaspoons baking
    powder
Salt
½ cup shortening
⅓ cup water
1 pound cooked pork,
    finely ground
1 cup mincemeat
½ teaspoon ground
    allspice
½ teaspoon ground
    nutmeg
½ teaspoon ground
    coriander
¼ cup piñon nuts
½ cup dark brown sugar
Oil for deep frying

Sift the flour with the baking powder and 1 teaspoon salt. Cut in the shortening with a pastry blender, add water and knead until the dough springs back when lightly pressed. Divide into 12 balls and roll out into circles ⅛ inch thick.

Prepare the filling by mixing the pork with the mincemeat, allspice, nutmeg, coriander, piñon nuts, brown sugar and salt to taste. If the filling appears too dry, add some corn syrup to hold it together but not so much that the filling becomes soft.

Put 1 heaping tablespoon of the filling in the center of the pastry. Moisten the edges of the circles with water, fold over, and press the edges together. Seal the pastry by pressing fork tines around the edges.

Deep fry until golden and drain on paper towels. These can also be baked at 400 degrees for about 20 minutes.

Note: Lean ground beef or a combination of beef and pork can be used if preferred.

FRUIT EMPANADAS   *MAKES 12*

1 cup dried fruit
½ cup sugar
¼ cup raisins
½ teaspoon ground
    cinnamon
¼ teaspoon ground
    nutmeg
¼ teaspoon ground
    cloves

Soak the fruit until soft and then simmer in a little water until very soft. Drain, mash the fruit, and add the spices. When the mixture is cool, make the empanadas following the directions in the recipe for Mincemeat Empanadas.

TUNA EMPANADAS

1 6½-ounce can tuna, drained
2 hard-boiled eggs, chopped
2 tablespoons chopped onion
¼ teaspoon chili powder
½ cup olive oil
½ cup light cream
Salt and pepper to taste

Mix all the ingredients together. Make the empanadas following the directions for Mincemeat Empanadas.

SPINACH EMPANADAS

1 cup cooked spinach, chopped
1 cup grated Cheddar cheese
6 bacon slices, cooked, crumbled
Ground nutmeg to taste

Mix all the ingredients together. Make the empanadas following the directions for Mincemeat Empanadas.

CHICKEN EMPANADAS

1 cup chopped cooked chicken
2 tablespoons chopped green onion
½ cup grated Cheddar cheese
1 clove garlic, minced
¼ teaspoon dried oregano
12 pimiento olives, chopped

Mix all the ingredients together. Make the empanadas following the directions for Mincemeat Empanadas.

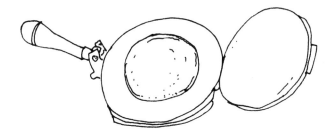

Burritos are enchiladas in white flour tortilla clothing. Mostly they are served with a pinto bean filling, but beef or pork can be used.

They are folded into neat packages, baked and served with a favorite sauce: chili, tomato, taco, or enchilada. Again, imagination is a basic ingredient.

PINTO BEAN BURRITOS MAKES 12

2 cloves garlic, minced
1 medium onion, chopped
2 tablespoons bacon fat or shortening
4 cups cooked pinto beans, mashed
  Salt
12 white flour tortillas (see p. 3)
  Oil for frying
1 cup chopped lettuce
3 tomatoes, chopped
1½ cups grated Cheddar cheese
2 cups chili sauce (see p. 59)

Sauté the garlic and onion in the bacon fat until tender. Add the beans and refry them, seasoning with salt to taste.

Prepare the tortillas by sprinkling with water and frying them quickly in the hot cooking oil until pliable.

Put a heaping tablespoon of the bean mixture in the center of each tortilla. Sprinkle with the chopped lettuce and tomato. Top with some grated cheese. Pour over some of the chili sauce and fold over the tortillas.

Bake at 350 degrees for 10 minutes. The burritos can be served with avocado slices and more of the chili sauce.

PORK BURRITOS MAKES 12

¼ onion, chopped
2 cups shredded cooked pork
1 tablespoon bacon fat or shortening
1 8-ounce can tomatoes, chopped
1 cup chopped green chilies
1 teaspoon salt
1 clove garlic, minced
12 white flour tortillas (see p. 3)
1 cup grated Cheddar cheese

Sauté the onion with the pork in the hot bacon fat until the onion is transparent.

Make a sauce combining the tomatoes, green chilies, salt, and garlic and heat for about 10 minutes.

Divide the meat mixture and wrap in the tortillas. Pour some chili sauce over the burritos and sprinkle with cheese.

Bake at 350 degrees until the cheese is melted.

BEEF AND BEAN BURRITOS

MAKES 12

1 pound ground lean beef
1 tablespoon bacon fat or shortening
1 medium onion, chopped
1 clove garlic, minced
2 stalks celery, chopped
1 cup chopped green chilies
2 cups cooked pinto beans, mashed
2 teaspoons salt
1 10-ounce can tomato sauce
12 white flour tortillas (see p. 3), warmed
1 cup grated Cheddar cheese

Brown the ground beef in the hot bacon fat. Drain off most of the fat and push the meat to one side of the pan. Add the onion and garlic and sauté until soft. Mix with the meat and add the celery, chilies, beans, salt, and tomato sauce. Simmer about 10 minutes so the liquid cooks down.

Place 1 heaping tablespoon of mixture on each warm tortilla and sprinkle with some cheese. Fold and top with more cheese.

Bake at 350 degrees until the cheese melts.

Note: For softer burritos, cover with foil or a lid. Garnish with lettuce.

BEEF JERKY BURRITOS

MAKES 12

3 cups water
1 10-ounce can green chilies
1 cup chopped onion
2 tablespoons cooking oil
1 cup chopped tomatoes
2 teaspoons salt
12 strips beef jerky (see next page)
12 white flour tortillas (see p. 3)
2 cups pinto beans, mashed

Bring the water to a boil and add the chilies. Remove from the heat and let stand for 10 minutes. Reserve the water. Remove the stems and seeds from the chilies and chop finely.

Sauté the onion in the cooking oil and add the tomatoes and salt.

Chop the jerky and combine it with the chili, onion-tomato mixture, and reserved water. Simmer for 1 hour, adding more hot water if necessary.

Stuff the warm tortillas with the mashed pinto beans and pour over the sauce.

51

BEEF JERKY

2 pounds top round
Salt
Pepper
Liquid smoke

Slice the meat in very fine strips, removing any fat. Make a ½-inch layer of beef in a stone crock. Sprinkle with salt, pepper, and liquid smoke. Repeat until all the beef is used up. Cover with foil and weight down. Leave overnight. Drain and dry on paper towels. Place the beef strips on racks in a 150-degree oven for 6 to 8 hours, depending on the degree of dryness desired.

Toasting Santa Fe with Margaritas, overlooking the Plaza.

A chili charmer at Rancho de Chimayo Restaurant with ristras in background.

Scrambled Eggs with Chorizo (p. 87)

1-b

A year round luncheon of Avocado Soup (p. 92) served hot or cold. Accompanied by Tamales (p. 35) and Pinto Bean Salad (p. 82)

Tacos and their ingredients (p. 31)

Kidney Beans, Posole, Chili Pequin Pods, Rice, Saffron, Pinto Beans.

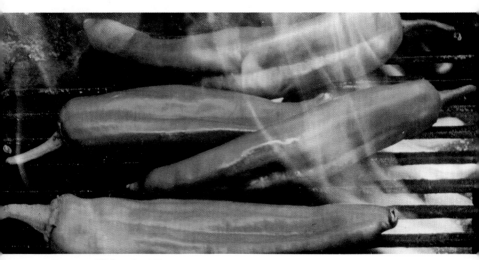

Chicos, Oregano, Cumin, Garbanzos, Ground Red Chili.

Roasting Chilies (p. 12)

1-d

CHILI RELLENOS

If a restaurant in Santa Fe serves perfectly prepared chili rellenos, its reputation is almost assured.

Meet the Prince, fresh or canned chili, stuffed with cheese or a well-seasoned meat mixture, and fried or baked in a batter until golden brown.

The chilies can be served as are, nestled inside the crisp batter, or topped with a tomato or chili salsa.

When in season, the best chilies for this dish are long and slender, easy to peel, and can be stuffed without breaking. Either green or red chilies may be used.

After peeling according to one of the methods in Chapter 3, the stems and seeds are removed. However, the seeds, or some of them at any rate, can be left intact for a hotter dish.

When stuffing with cheese, the Cheddar, Longhorn, or Monterey Jack—whichever the preference—can be grated, cubed, or cut into slices, the latter probably being the more classic way to do it.

Out of season, canned chilies, peeled and whole, may be used without impairing the flavor of this superb dish.

CHILI
RELLENOS CON QUESO   *MAKES 12*

12 long, slender green
    chilies
1 pound Cheddar
    cheese, cut in slices
1½ cups all-purpose flour
1 teaspoon salt
    Pepper to taste
1 cup milk
1 tablespoon cooking oil
2 eggs, slightly beaten
    Oil for frying
1 cup red or green chili
    sauce (see pp. 59-61)

Peel the chilies, open a small slit below stems and remove seeds, if desired. Stuff with strips of the cheese. Be careful not to break the chilies.

Prepare the batter by mixing the flour, salt, and pepper. Blend in the milk, cooking oil and slightly beaten eggs. Combine and stir enough to mix. Let stand, covered, for 2 hours.

Roll the stuffed chilies in the batter and deep fry in hot oil until golden brown. Serve with the chili sauce. Excellent with Spanish rice or refried beans.

BAKED CHILI RELLENOS   *MAKES 12*

12 long, slender green
    chilies
1 pound Cheddar
    cheese, cut in slices
4 eggs, separated
¾ teaspoon baking
    powder
4 tablespoons all-purpose
    flour
¼ teaspoon salt

Prepare and stuff the chilies as in the recipe for Chili Rellenos Con Queso. Place in a greased casserole.

Beat the egg whites until stiff. Beat the yolks until thick. Sift together the dry ingredients and add to the yolks, blending well. Fold the beaten whites into the yolk mixture.

Pour the batter over the stuffed chilies and bake at 325 degrees until the batter is done and lightly browned on top. Serve at once garnished with chopped lettuce and tomatoes, if desired.

Note: For a variation, put a teaspoon of minced onion along with the cheese in each chili.

CHILI
RELLENOS IN SAUCE
MAKES 12

12 long, slender green
    chilies
1½ pounds Cheddar
    cheese, cut in slices
1 medium onion, chopped
2 cloves garlic, minced
2 tablespoons cooking oil
1 1-pound can tomatoes,
    chopped
1 cup chicken stock
1 tablespoon chili
    powder
½ teaspoon dried oregano
¼ teaspoon ground cumin
    Salt and pepper to taste

Prepare and stuff the chili as for Chili Rellenos Con Queso. Place in a shallow baking pan and put another strip of cheese on top of each pepper.

Sauté the onion and garlic in the hot oil until transparent. Stir in the remaining ingredients and simmer for 10 to 15 minutes.

Pour the sauce over the chilies and bake at 350 degrees until the cheese is melted.

CHILI
RELLENOS CON CARNE
MAKES 12

1 pound lean ground
    beef
1 small onion, chopped
1 clove garlic, minced
2 tablespoons cooking oil
1 teaspoon salt
2 teaspoons mild chili
    powder
1 6-ounce can tomato
    paste
½ teaspoon dried oregano
¼ teaspoon ground cumin
½ cup raisins
12 long, slender green
    chilies
    Batter
    Oil for frying

Brown the beef, onion, and garlic in the hot oil. Add the salt, chili powder, tomato paste, oregano, cumin, and raisins and simmer for 10 minutes, or until well blended. Adjust the seasonings if needed.

Prepare the chilies and stuff with the meat mixture. Dip them in the batter (see either Chili Rellenos Con Queso, or Baked Chili Rellenos) and fry in the cooking oil, 2 at a time, until golden brown. A tomato sauce is good with this dish.

SAUCES, DIPS, AND RELISHES

As mentioned earlier, purists just won't add tomatoes to chili, contending that the love fruit alters the taste of good chili.

However, they do consent to making a cold salsa (sauce) with both. Chili sauce is basic to many recipes and it can be made from green or red chili, either fresh, canned, frozen or dried.

Fresh green chili sauce is made with tomato and in most homes a large container of the salsa is kept in back of the refrigerator for immediate use on eggs, hamburgers and meats of all kinds. It keeps well under cover for four or five days.

Green chili is peeled and then the stems, seeds and veins are removed. For a hotter sauce, some or all of the seeds and veins can be left in. An addition of vinegar will make a tart sauce, while some olive oil will reduce the pungency.

Fresh red chili is not peeled. After the stems, seeds and veins are removed, the chilies are boiled and then put in a blender to make a smooth paste.

Whole dry red pods or chili powder can also be used in making red chili sauce. Toasting the pods before blending or grinding is optional. The pods are put through a ricer or colander to separate the pulp from the tough outer skin, or they can be put in an electric blender to blend the pulp and skin to a smooth paste. The sauce can then be strained or not, depending on taste.

The chili pods can be covered with hot water, brought to a boil and taken off the heat to steep for an hour. Or the pods can be boiled for 10 to 15 minutes before separating the pulp from the skins. The pulp must be soft to separate easily from the skin.

The pungency is largely in the veins of the chili—the amount to be removed is a personal choice.

Everything, then, is a matter of choice, experience, and imagination, and, when bottled, it's worth a fortune to a dulled palate.

The same holds true for the dips and relishes included on these pages that can make a dinner party or buffet a memorable occasion, at least, until the next one.

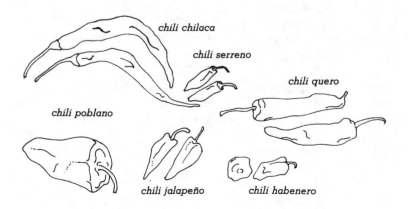

chili chilaca

chili serreno

chili quero

chili poblano

chili jalapeño

chili habenero

FRESH GREEN CHILI SAUCE

MAKES ABOUT 1 CUP

12 green chilies
1 ripe tomato
1 clove garlic, pressed
½ teaspoon salt
1 medium onion,
    chopped

Peel the chilies and remove the stems, seeds, and veins as desired.

Peel the tomato after covering it with boiling water for 15 to 20 seconds. Then mash the tomato until it is almost a liquid. Chop the chili very finely and combine it with the tomato. Add the garlic, salt, and onion. This is a good, basic sauce for tacos, enchiladas, chili rellenos and even as a hot dip.

SWEET CHILI SAUCE

MAKES ABOUT 3 QUARTS

5 pounds small ripe
    tomatoes
4 green chilies, peeled
    and chopped
1 red chili pod, chopped
4 onions, chopped
1 tablespoon salt
½ teaspoon ground
    ginger
6 tablespoons dark
    brown sugar
1 teaspoon ground
    cinnamon
3 cups cider vinegar

Mash the tomatoes, chilies, and onions together. Add the salt, ginger, brown sugar, and cinnamon.

Boil the mixture for about 2 hours, or until tender and blended. Add the cider vinegar and boil for another 5 minutes. Pour into sterilized jars and seal immediately. This is a good relish to serve with beans, with lettuce in a sandwich and on corn chips as an appetizer.

FRESH RED CHILI SAUCE

MAKES ABOUT 1 ½ CUPS

20 fresh red chilies (or 1 cup frozen red chilies)
1 teaspoon salt
1 clove garlic, chopped
1 small onion, sliced
1 teaspoon dried oregano
½ cup water
1 tablespoon butter or or margarine

Prepare the chilies by removing the stems, seeds, and veins. Cover with boiling water and let stand for 10 minutes. Remove the chilies and place in a blender with the salt, garlic, onion, and oregano. Add water according to blender instructions and blend until all ingredients are reduced to a smooth paste.

Transfer the sauce to a heavy pan and add the ½ cup water (more or less depending on the amount used in the blending). Add the butter and simmer for about 30 minutes, or until the mixture has the desired consistency, about that of tomato sauce. Stir occasionally to keep from burning. This can be frozen and is excellent as a base in recipes for tacos, enchiladas, burritos, and chili.

RED CHILI POWDER SAUCE

MAKES ABOUT 2 CUPS

3 tablespoons shortening
2 tablespoons all-purpose flour
1 clove garlic, chopped
½ cup chili powder
2 cups water
1 teaspoon salt

Melt the shortening, blend in the flour and garlic, and cook until mixed well. Add the chili powder, water, and salt and stir over moderate heat until completely combined. Chili burns very easily. The quality of the sauce depends on the quality and type of chili powder.

DRIED RED CHILI SAUCE

20 dried red chili pods
1 quart hot water
¼ cup onion, chopped
1 clove garlic, chopped
1 tablespoon fat or
  shortening
1 teaspoon salt
1 teaspoon dried oregano

Remove the stems, seeds, and veins from the chili. Wash in warm water. Put them in a pan and cover with the hot water. Bring almost to a boil and remove the pan from the heat. Let the chilies stand in the water for an hour, or until the pulp separates readily from the skins. Put through a food mill or colander, adding enough of the water the pods were cooked in to remove the pulp. If sauce is very thick, thin with water.

Sauté the onion and garlic in the shortening until tender. Add the chili, salt and oregano and bring to a boil.

TACO SAUCE

4 tablespoons shortening
2 tablespoons all-purpose
  flour
1 medium onion,
  chopped
2 cloves garlic, minced
2 tomatoes, chopped
1 cup chopped green
  chilies, or ¼ cup
  chili powder, or to
  taste
2 cups water
1 teaspoon salt

Heat the shortening in a large skillet and add the flour, onion and garlic. Blend well until brown. Stir in the tomatoes and chili (or chili powder). Simmer while slowly adding the water. Add the salt and cook until thick. For a thicker sauce, add more water mixed with flour. Also good on burritos, chili rellenos, and other dishes.

ENCHILADA SAUCE
MAKES 1 CUP

1 11-ounce container frozen red chilies
½ cup water
2 cloves garlic, chopped
½ teaspoon salt
2 tablespoons shortening
1 tablespoon all-purpose flour

Combine the chili, water, garlic, and salt and bring to a boil. Blend in the shortening and flour and simmer for 15 minutes, adding more hot water if sauce becomes too thick.

TOMATO ENCHILADA SAUCE
MAKES ABOUT 4 CUPS

1 medium onion, chopped
2 tablespoons bacon fat or cooking oil
½ cup chopped green chilies
6 tablespoons chili powder
4 tomatoes, peeled and chopped
1 teaspoon salt
2 cups chicken stock

Sauté the onion in the hot fat. Add the chilies, chili powder, tomatoes, and salt. Mix well and simmer for 15 minutes. Put the mixture in a blender and purée. Reheat with the chicken stock.

MEAT ENCHILADA SAUCE
MAKES ABOUT 6 CUPS

2 pounds lean ground beef or pork
2 tablespoons cooking oil
2 tablespoons all-purpose flour
¼ cup chili powder
6 cups water
2 teaspoons salt
2 teaspoons garlic powder

Brown the meat in the oil in a large saucepan. Pour off most of the fat. Combine the flour and chili powder and add to the meat. Slowly add the water and simmer until thick. Season with the salt and garlic powder and cook until well blended. Some of the sauce can be frozen.

CHICKEN ENCHILADA SAUCE

2 cups chicken stock
  (or 1 can soup and 1
  can water or milk)
3 tablespoons chili
  powder
1 clove garlic, chopped
½ teaspoon ground cumin
  Salt to taste
1 tablespoon cornstarch
2 tablespoons water

Combine the stock, chili powder, garlic, cumin, and salt and bring to a boil. Mix the cornstarch with the water and add to the chili mixture. Boil for 1 minute.

CHILI CON QUESO

1 medium onion,
  chopped
1 clove garlic, minced
2 tablespoons butter or
  vegetable oil
1 cup green chili sauce
  (see p. 59)
½ cup heavy cream or
  evaporated milk
½ pound process cheese,
  chopped
  Corn chips

Sauté the onion and garlic until tender. Add the green chili sauce and bring to a boil. Remove from heat and add the cream and cheese. Stir to blend all flavors and heat gently until the cheese melts. This can be done in a double boiler to keep it from scorching. Keep warm in a skillet or chafing dish. Serve with corn chips (tostados). Classic dish at parties.

GREEN CHILI DIP

6 fresh or canned green
  chilies
1 16-ounce package
  cream cheese
  Corn chips

Peel the chilies and remove the stems, seeds, and veins. Chop fine. Bring the cream cheese to room temperature and blend with the chilies. This dip is good with corn chips, potato chips, celery and carrot sticks.

HAM-CHILI DIP *MAKES ABOUT 2 CUPS*

½ cup green chili sauce
(see p. 59)
1 can deviled ham (or 1
cup chopped
bologna, wieners,
ham)
½ cup cottage cheese

Blend all the ingredients until smooth. Serve with chips or crackers.

AVOCADO-CHILI DIP *MAKES ABOUT 2 CUPS*

12 green chilies, peeled
and chopped
1 clove garlic, minced
3 tablespoons French
dressing
3 ripe avocados, mashed
3 tablespoons milk
1 16-ounce package
cream cheese

Mix all the ingredients to a creamy consistency and serve either as an appetizer or salad.

GUACAMOLE DIP *MAKES ABOUT 2 CUPS*

2 avocados, mashed
1 tomato, peeled and
chopped
¼ cup sour cream
2 teaspoons salt
1 fresh green chili,
peeled and chopped
1 clove garlic, minced
2 teaspoons lemon or
lime juice
2 tablespoons chopped
onion
⅛ teaspoon Tabasco
Corn chips

Mix all the ingredients together, cover, and chill. Serve with chips.

PINTO BEAN DIP

1 cup cooked drained
   pinto beans, mashed
1 cup ketchup
2 tablespoons chopped
   onion
2 fresh green chilies,
   peeled and chopped
½ teaspoon salt
   Dash of Tabasco
   Horseradish to taste
1 tablespoon lemon
   juice

Mash the pinto beans well and combine with the ketchup. Add the remaining ingredients and mix well.

GREEN CHILI RELISH

12 fresh green chilies
2 cloves garlic, minced
1 small onion, chopped
   Salt to taste

Peel the chilies and remove the stems, seeds, and veins. Chop the chilies finely and add the garlic, onion, and salt.

BEAN RELISH

½ cup chopped green
   chilies
½ cup minced onion
1 cup cooked drained
   pinto beans
¼ cup white vinegar
2 tablespoons sugar
2 teaspoons celery seed
   Salt to taste

Combine all the ingredients and mix well. Refrigerate to blend flavors. This is excellent with cold meat.

PICKLED JALAPEÑOS   *MAKES 1 QUART*

White vinegar
Water
2½ dozen jalapeño
    peppers
Salad oil
1 large onion, chopped
1 clove garlic, minced
1 teaspoon cumin seed
1 teaspoon ground
    coriander
2 teaspoons salt

To make the pickling solution, mix equal amounts of vinegar and water. Bring solution to a boil and allow to cool.

Wash the chilies and pat dry with a soft cloth.

Cover the bottom of a large skillet with the salad oil. Add the onion, garlic, cumin seed, and coriander. Heat the chilies in the spicy fat until the skins begin to blister.

Pack while hot in sterilized jars, adding 1 teaspoon of salt for each pint of peppers. Cover with the pickling solution and add a teaspoon of the oil-spice mixture. Seal and let stand for at least 1 month before using.

OTHER SPECIALTIES

Besides the aforementioned specialties, there are other main dishes in Santa Fe cookery incorporating beef, pork, chicken, pinto beans, or chili peppers—cut up, mixed up, added to other ingredients and served as a one-of-a-kind dish by the imaginative cook.

Chili again is used liberally in chicken dishes, on top of pan fried steak, in spaghetti sauce, wherever the cook decides to add a little spice to an otherwise "bland" dish.

Steaks, chops, and roasts really aren't traditional Santa Fe dishes—even though they are available in restaurants and served in the home—the trick is to add just that extra touch of seasoning or another ingredient or two to make the dish something different, "Oh, what Carmen made the other night!"

The name of the game obviously is experimentation, if only to put some chopped chili on a scrambled egg or slice of liver. The following recipes, then, can be taken with a grain of salt or not.

CHILI CHICKEN

SERVES 4

1 3-pound chicken, cut
    into serving pieces
1 clove garlic, peeled
1 teaspoon salt
1 medium onion, minced
2 tablespoons fat
1 cup green chili sauce
    (see p. 59)

Simmer the chicken in a small amount of water with the garlic and salt until tender, about 30 minutes.

Sauté the onion in the hot fat until transparent. Add the chili sauce and bring to a boil. Pour over the cooked chicken and simmer for another 30 minutes.

CHILI VEAL STEAK

SERVES 4

2 pounds veal steak,
    cut into serving
    pieces
3 tablespoons all-
    purpose flour
1 tablespoon chili
    powder
½ teaspoon salt
4 tablespoons bacon fat
    or oil
1 medium onion,
    chopped
1 cup sour cream
1 clove garlic, pressed

Dredge the veal cut into serving pieces in a mixture of the flour, chili powder, and salt. Brown the meat in the hot fat. Add the onion, sour cream, and garlic. Transfer to a baking dish, cover, and bake at 325 degrees for about 1 hour, or until the meat is tender.

Note: Round steak or lean pork can be substituted for the veal, but use 1 cup chopped fresh chili instead of chili powder.

PINTO BEAN LOAF

1 small onion, minced
2 tablespoons bacon fat or oil
2 cups cooked pinto beans, mashed
2 eggs, beaten
1 cup bread crumbs
Salt and pepper
½ cup milk
4 bacon strips
Minced parsley

Fry the onion in the hot fat until tender. Mix in the mashed pinto beans. Remove from the heat and stir in the beaten eggs, bread crumbs, salt and pepper to taste, and the milk to moisten. Shape into a loaf and place in a greased loaf pan. Put the strips of bacon on top.

Bake at 350 degrees for 45 to 50 minutes. Garnish with the parsley and serve with a hot tomato or mushroom sauce as desired. One can of condensed tomato or cream of mushroom soup makes an excellent well-seasoned sauce.

EGGPLANT AND CHILI

1 large eggplant, peeled and cubed
1 small onion, chopped
1 egg, beaten
2 cups bread crumbs
1 cup chopped green chilies
6 strips bacon
Salt and pepper

Cook the eggplant in salted water until tender. Drain well, cool, and then mash. Combine the onion, egg, bread crumbs, chilies, and salt and pepper to taste. Add to the eggplant and mix well. Pour into a greased 9x9x2-inch casserole, place the bacon strips side by side on top and bake at 350 degrees for 45 minutes.

(Breakfast Sausage)
CHORIZO
MAKES ABOUT 24

1 pound lean ground
   beef
1 pound pork sausage
2 cloves garlic, minced
1 small onion, minced
3 tablespoons chili
   powder
3 tablespoons white
   vinegar
1 teaspoon dried oregano
1 teaspoon salt
¼ teaspoon ground
   cloves (optional)
½ teaspoon ground
   cinnamon (optional)

Mix all the ingredients and refrigerate for 4 hours. Make patties or roll into little sausages. Brown well in an ungreased skillet.

POSOLE STEW
SERVES 4 TO 6

2 pounds lean pork,
   cubed
1 quart water for
   cooking
1 teaspoon salt
2½ pounds posole
   (or chicos)
4 cloves garlic, minced
3 red chili pods, chop-
   ped or 2 tablespoons
   chili powder
½ teaspoon dried oregano

Boil the pork in salted water until tender. Add the posole, garlic, chilies, and oregano and simmer in a heavy covered pot until the hominy kernels are bursting and soft. This is excellent either by itself or as a side dish.

CHICKEN TORTILLA PIE

1 onion, chopped
1 tablespoon cooking oil
1 cup chopped fresh
   green chilies
1 can cream of chicken
   soup
1 can cream of
   mushroom soup
1 can chicken broth or
   stock
12 corn tortillas, cut in
   strips
1 broiler chicken,
   cooked and boned
½ pound Cheddar
   cheese, cut in strips

Sauté the onion in the oil until tender and then mix thoroughly with the chili, soups, and broth.

In a greased 9 x 9 x 2 - inch casserole, alternate layers of tortilla strips, chicken, chili sauce, and slices of cheese. Repeat process until all the ingredients are used up.

Bake at 350 degrees for about 45 minutes.

(Chicken with Rice)
ARROZ CON POLLO

1 4-pound fryer, cut
   into pieces
2 teaspoons salt
   Pepper to taste
¼ cup olive oil
1 onion, chopped
1 clove garlic, minced
3 cups canned tomatoes
   with liquid
½ teaspoon dried oregano
12 ripe olives, sliced
1 bay leaf
1 tablespoon red chili
   powder
2 cups water
1 cup rice
1 package frozen peas
   Strips of pimiento

Season the cut-up chicken with half the salt and pepper to taste. Brown the chicken in the hot oil and set aside.

Sauté the onion and garlic until tender in the same oil and then add the tomatoes, the remaining salt, oregano, olives, bay leaf, chili powder, and water. Bring to a boil. Put in the chicken and rice. Cover tightly and simmer for 25 minutes without lifting the lid.

When done, sprinkle in the peas, cover, and cook another few minutes, or until the peas are tender. Garnish with strips of pimiento.

CHILAQUILES

8 stale tortillas
4 tablespoons bacon fat
1 medium onion,
   chopped
2 cloves garlic, minced
1 pound lean ground
   beef
2 ripe tomatoes, mashed
½ cup chopped green
   chilies
1 teaspoon salt
1 cup water
½ pound Cheddar
   cheese, grated

Slice the stale tortillas into eighths and fry in the hot fat. Drain. Sauté the onion and garlic in the same fat until tender. Add the beef and brown. Stir in the tomatoes, chilies, salt and water, bring to a boil and simmer gently for 5 minutes.

Place the tortilla wedges in a baking dish and cover with the cheese. Pour over the sauce and bake at 350 degrees for about 5 minutes. Garnish with shredded lettuce, if desired, and serve in individual pieces.

GREEN CHILI CASSEROLE

3 4-ounce cans whole
   green chilies,
   peeled
1 teaspoon salt
6 eggs, beaten
½ pound Cheddar
   cheese grated
¼ cup milk

Slit the chili pods lengthwise and line a greased 9x9x2-inch casserole covering the sides as well as the bottom. Salt lightly.

Mix the eggs, cheese, and milk and pour over the chilies.

Bake at 350 degrees for about 30 minutes, or until the casserole is set. Serve in squares on crackers either as a spicy appetizer or as an entrée.

MARINATED PORK

16 red chili pods
1 quart boiling water
¼ cup chopped onion
4 cloves garlic, minced
2 tablespoons dried oregano
1 tablespoon salt
5 pounds lean pork, cut in strips
Oil for frying

Remove the stems, seeds, and veins from the chili. Wash in warm water. Put them in a pan and cover with the boiling water and remove the pan from the heat. Let the chili stand for 1 hour, or until the pulp separates easily from the skins. Put through a food mill or colander, adding enough of the water the pods were cooked in to remove the pulp. If sauce is very thick, thin with water. Add the onion, garlic, oregano, and salt. Mix well.

Put the strips of the pork in the sauce and let sit for 24 hours. To cook, remove as many strips as needed and cut into bite-sized pieces. Fry in some hot fat covered by some chili sauce until done. The strips may also be baked at 350 degrees for 1 hour.

TRIPE (Menudo)

3 pounds tripe, chopped
1 quart lightly salted water
1 large onion, chopped
1 clove garlic, minced
4 tablespoons cooking oil
¼ cup chopped green chilies
2 teaspoons salt
2 teaspoons dried oregano
12 pimiento-stuffed green olives, sliced

Wash the tripe and cut into 2-inch squares. Simmer in a covered pot in the water for 1 hour.

Sauté the onion and garlic in the hot oil in a large skillet until tender. Add the chilies, salt, and oregano. Drain the tripe and add to the mixture. Cover and cook until the tripe is tender. Garnish with the olives and serve very hot.

VEGETABLES

While the Spaniards may have introduced wheat, goats, pigs, cattle, and sheep to the New World, they found upon arriving an abundance of native vegetables which continue to be staples in Santa Fe cookery.

They are: the pinto bean, corn, squash, chili pepper, and tomato, and to some extent, although they are more southern in nature, the pumpkin, eggplant, avocado, jicama, and potato. It is thought that the potato originated in South America.

Jicama is a root vegetable which is often eaten raw in salads. Its flavor falls somewhere between that of a crisp apple and a Chinese water chestnut.

Dried kernels of corn are called chicos and are available in all markets in New Mexico and by mail. They can be used in place of dry posole in posole stew.

As with pinto beans, they are soaked overnight or until the kernels are swollen. Then, basically, they can be cooked with a little sugar, if desired, until tender and seasoned with salt and chili.

Chili can add zest to many vegetables. Right at serving time, fresh, crisp chili, with seeds and membranes removed and shredded very finely, can be added to green beans, braised cabbage, buttered carrots, cauliflower, turnips, and the like. The chili need not be peeled.

(Chili con Papas)
BREAKFAST POTATOES *SERVES 6 TO 8*

Oil for frying
3 boiled potatoes, diced
1 cup chopped green
   chilies
Salt to taste

Heat the oil or bacon fat and fry the potatoes with the chilies until well browned. Salt and serve piping hot.

Note: Onions can be a nice addition.

CHICOS *SERVES 6*

2 cups chicos
4 cups water
1 teaspoon sugar
2 teaspoons salt
3 red chili pods,
   crushed
2 tablespoons butter

Wash and rinse the chicos. Cover and soak overnight, or until the kernels are swollen. Add the sugar, making sure the chicos are always covered with water, and bring to a boil. Simmer for 1 hour and then add the salt, chili, and butter (or use salt pork for a truer flavor). Continue cooking for another 2 hours.

BAKED CORN *SERVES 6*

1 onion, minced
1 tablespoon bacon fat
   or oil
3 cups uncooked corn
½ cup chopped fresh
   green chilies
2 tablespoons butter
2 cups tomato paste
Salt to taste

Sauté the onion in the hot fat until transparent. Mix the remaining ingredients together and add to the onion. Put into a buttered 1-quart soufflé dish and bake at 350 degrees for 1 hour.

CHILI CORN

½ pound bacon, diced
½ cup chopped fresh
   green chilies
1 large can creamed-
   style corn
2 eggs, beaten
Salt

Fry the bacon until crisp. Pour off all but a little of the fat and add the chilies, corn, and eggs. Season with salt to taste. Cook slowly until the eggs are creamy and thickened.

SERVES 6

CHILI CABBAGE

8 strips bacon
4 cups cooked cabbage,
   chopped
½ cup chopped fresh
   green chilies
Salt to taste

Fry the bacon. Crumble and return to the pan with the remaining ingredients. Mix and heat in the same fat.

BEAN AND
SERVES 6 TO 8   CARROT CASSEROLE

2 cups cooked drained
   pinto beans
2 cups cooked cubed
   carrots
½ cup finely chopped
   celery leaves
   Lemon juice
1 teaspoon salt
   Pepper to taste
½ cup bread crumbs,
   sautéed in
2 tablespoons butter

In a greased casserole, alternate layers of pinto beans and carrots. Sprinkle the carrots with the celery leaves and a little lemon juice. Season with salt and pepper to taste. Pour the liquid in which the carrots were cooked over the last layer and top with the bread crumbs. Bake at 350 degrees until well heated and brown on top.

PINTO BEANS AND RICE

SERVES 8

2 ounces salt pork
2 cups cooked undrained pinto beans
2 onions, chopped
2 teaspoons salt
  Pepper to taste
1½ cups cooked rice

Cut the salt pork into ⅛-inch cubes and brown in a skillet. Add the cubes to the beans. Brown the onions in the salt pork fat, mix with the beans and season with the salt and pepper to taste. Combine the beans with the rice and continue cooking for 10 minutes. Serve immediately. If desired, sprinkle with grated cheese and serve with a tomato sauce.

MEXICAN RICE

SERVES 4 TO 6

1 onion, chopped
1 clove garlic, minced
¼ cup cooking oil
1 cup uncooked rice
2 cups boiling chicken stock
1 tablespoon chopped parsley
1 teaspoon salt
  Pepper to taste

Sauté the onion and garlic in the hot oil until transparent. Add the rice and sauté until the rice is coated with oil and turns golden. Add more oil if necessary to make sure every grain is coated and then drain any excess fat, if any, when the rice is yellow.

Transfer to a 2-quart saucepan and add the broth, parsley, salt, and pepper to taste. Cover tightly and simmer for 20 minutes without lifting the lid. This is served on a combination plate or with any main course.

BAKED
RICE AND CHILI

SERVES 4 TO 6

1 cup chopped green
   chilies
2 cups sour cream
2 cups cooked rice
1 teaspoon salt
   Pepper to taste
½ teaspoon dried oregano
½ pound process cheese,
   grated

Mix the chilies and sour cream together. Season the rice with the salt, pepper to taste, and oregano.

In a greased 1-quart soufflé dish, alternate layers of rice, chili-sour cream mixture and cheese, ending up with rice and reserving some of the cheese.

Bake at 350 degrees for 30 minutes. Put the remaining cheese on top and continue heating until it melts.

GREEN CHILI
AND SQUASH

SERVES 6 TO 8

12 green chilies, or ½
   cup frozen chilies
1 small onion, chopped
1 clove garlic, minced
1 tablespoon bacon fat
   or cooking oil
2 cups cubed summer
   squash
1 cup fresh or frozen
   corn
1 teaspoon salt
   Pepper to taste
½ cup water (if necessary)
½ cup grated Cheddar
   cheese

Prepare the chilies by removing stems, seeds, and veins, and peeling if desired. Sauté the onion and garlic slightly in the hot fat. Add the squash and cook until tender. When done, add the chili, corn, salt, pepper to taste, and water, if necessary, and simmer for 10 to 15 minutes. Top with the cheese and continue heating until melted.

CHILI AND EGGPLANT
SERVES 6

2 medium onions,
   chopped
3 tablespoons bacon fat
   or cooking oil
1 medium eggplant,
   peeled and cubed
6 fresh green chilies,
   peeled and chopped
2 medium tomatoes,
   chopped
2 teaspoons salt
   Pepper to taste

Sauté the onion in the hot fat until tender. Add the eggplant, chilies, and tomatoes. Season with the salt and pepper to taste. Cover and simmer for about 20 minutes.

CHILI TOMATOES
SERVES 4

4 large ripe tomatoes
½ cup chopped fresh
   green chilies
½ cup bread crumbs
1 clove garlic, minced
   Salt to taste
4 thin slices butter

Cut the tops off the tomatoes and hollow out the insides, reserving the pulp. Drain the pulp well and mix with the chilies, bread crumbs, garlic, and salt.

Stuff the tomatoes with the mixture and top each with a slice of butter.

Bake at 350 degrees for 15 to 20 minutes, or until thoroughly heated.

(Quelites) PINTO BEANS AND SPINACH
SERVES 4

¼ cup onion, chopped
2 tablespoons bacon fat
2 cups cooked spinach,
   chopped
½ cup cooked drained
   pinto beans
1 teaspoon red chili
   powder
1 teaspoon salt

Sauté the onion in the hot fat or oil until tender. Add all the other ingredients and cook for 5 minutes, or until all the flavors are blended.

SALADS

It is often the case a meal does not call for a salad, what with all that chopped tomato, shredded lettuce, and slices of avocado atop, around and in the tacos, enchiladas, tostadas, and the rest. There are these particular luncheons, dinners, or buffets where a salad is served singly, as an accompaniment or as something to put out the fire, such as an avocado salad after blazing hot chili.

Fresh green chili, itself, need not be peeled, merely finely shredded, when being added to salads and dressings.

The pinto bean again plays a part in salads in Santa Fe. The variations are limited only by one's imagination.

PINTO BEAN SALAD *SERVES 6*

2 cups cooked drained
    pinto beans
1 cup diced celery
1 medium onion,
    chopped
4 tablespoons salad
    dressing (see p. 84)
3 fresh green chilies,
    chopped
1 cup crumbled white
    cheese
  Salt to taste
  Lettuce leaves

Mix all the ingredients, except the lettuce, and moisten with the salad dressing. Chill. Serve on lettuce leaves with more dressing. Add or substitute cucumber slices, avocado, chopped pickle, bacon bits, carrot cubes, canned peas, or chopped hard-boiled eggs.

HOT POTATO SALAD *SERVES 6 TO 8*

3 large potatoes,
    cooked, peeled, and
    diced
2 teaspoons salt
½ cup chopped fresh
    green chilies
¼ cup chopped carrots
¼ cup chopped celery
1 large onion, chopped
½ cup chopped pickles
½ cup cider vinegar
4 hard-boiled eggs,
    chopped

Season the potatoes with the salt and add the chilies, carrots, celery, onion, and pickles. Moisten with the cider vinegar and add the eggs. Serve hot.

CHILI
COTTAGE CHEESE SALAD *SERVES 4*

1 cup cottage cheese
½ cup chopped green
    chilies
¼ cup mayonnaise
½ cup chopped onion
  Lettuce leaves

Combine the cottage cheese, chili, mayonnaise, and onion and serve on the lettuce leaves.

CHILI COLESLAW

1 medium cabbage,
   shredded
1 cup chopped green
   chilies
1 medium onion,
   chopped
2 tablespoons lemon
   juice
2 teaspoons salt
1 teaspoon celery seed
⅓ cup white vinegar
⅓ cup water
⅓ cup olive oil
1 teaspoon sugar

Combine the cabbage, chili, and onion. Sprinkle with the lemon juice and toss. Season with the salt and celery seed. Make a dressing with the vinegar, water, olive oil, and sugar. Pour over salad and refrigerate for at least 1 hour before serving.

AVOCADO AND TOMATO SALAD

3 ripe avocados,
   peeled and diced
2 tablespoons lemon
   juice
3 tomatoes, chopped
1 onion, chopped
2 teaspoons salt
1 teaspoon chili powder
   Lettuce leaves
1 cup French dressing (see p. 84)

Combine the avocados which have been sprinkled with lemon juice to retain their color, tomatoes, onion, salt, and chili powder. Chill. Divide and serve on lettuce leaves. Pour the dressing over each.

AVOCADO AND ORANGE SALAD

2 large avocados,
   peeled and sliced
3 large oranges, peeled
   and sliced
1 purple onion, peeled
   and sliced
   Lettuce leaves
1 cup French dressing
   Tarragon to taste

Alternate slices of the avocados, oranges, and onion on top of the lettuce leaves. Douse with the dressing and add the tarragon to taste.

MUSTARD DRESSING   *MAKES ¼ CUP*

1 tablespoon prepared
   mustard
3 tablespoons cream

Beat the mustard and cream until blended. This is excellent to blend in with a pinto bean mixture for a salad.

CHILI
FRENCH DRESSING   *MAKES 1 CUP*

⅔ cup olive oil
⅓ cup vinegar
1 teaspoon salt
   Pepper to taste
1 clove garlic (optional)
2 tablespoons chopped
   green chilies, or
2 tablespoons chili
   sauce, or
½ teaspoon red chili
   powder

Combine the olive oil, vinegar (alter ratio to suit taste), salt, pepper, and garlic. Add the chili, blend and chill thoroughly.

THOUSAND
ISLAND DRESSING   *MAKES 1½ CUPS*

1 cup mayonnaise
½ cup chopped green
   chilies, or
⅓ cup chili sauce
2 tablespoons chopped
   pimiento-stuffed
   olives
1 teaspoon chives,
   chopped

Combine all the ingredients and chill before serving.

Many of the ingredients that go into SANTA FE COOKERY.

Essentials to any party: Bean Dip (p. 65), Chili con Queso (p. 63), Guacamole (p. 64) with Corn Chips (p. 4), and Sliced Jicama (p. 75) served on Santa Fe Trays.

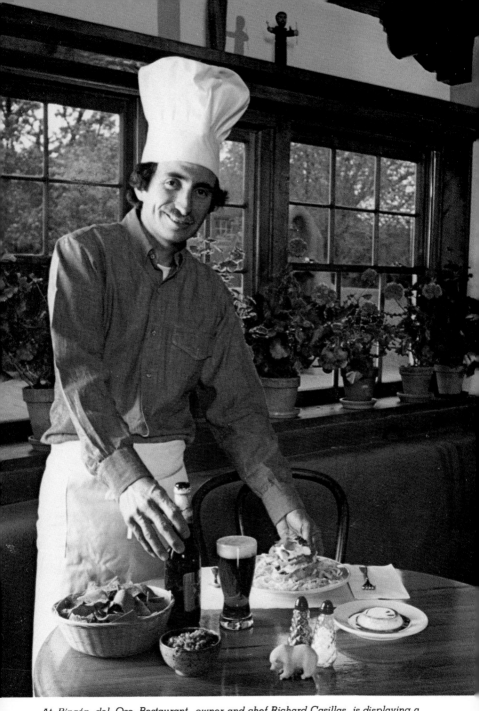

At Rincón del Oso Restaurant, owner and chef Richard Casillas, is displaying a Chalupa (p. 42) and Flan (p. 108) prepared by his wife, Debby Casillas.

An elegant finale of Cinnamon Peaches (p. 110) and Hot Chocolate (p. 113).

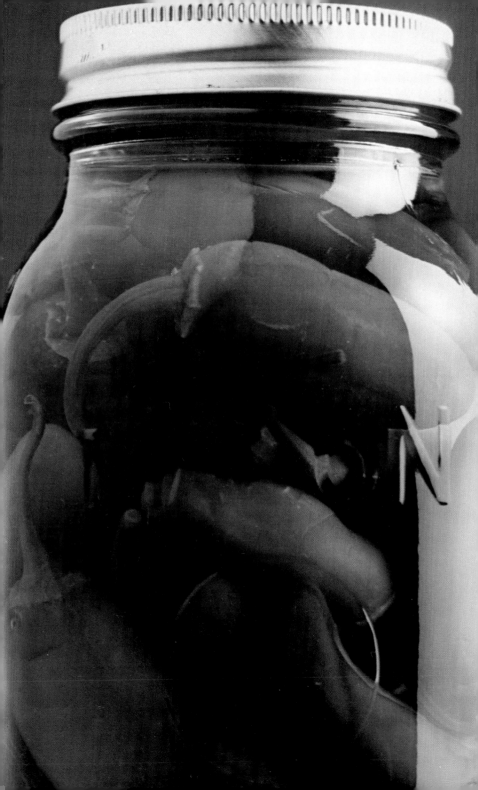

EGGS

Eggs take on a regal quality in Santa Fe cookery. Set in a velvet green or red chili sauce, they are the center of attraction accompanied by consorts of tomatoes, onions, avocado, and chorizo (Spanish sausage).

An egg may be just an egg elsewhere, but a green chili omelette or a plate of huevos rancheros is a feast any time, whether it be at breakfast, lunch, or four in the morning.

Huevos rancheros (ranch-style eggs), by now, is a world dish, but the variations of preparing it indicate the use of the egg in New Mexico. In this form, the eggs can be fried or poached, in a chili sauce or separately, and they can be served on warm tortillas or the tortillas can be served on the side, whichever.

Pickled Jalapeños (p.66)

HUEVOS RANCHEROS

SERVES 4

4 cups green or red
  chili sauce
  (see pp. 59-61)
8 eggs
8 warm tortillas
1 cup grated Cheddar
  cheese

Heat the chili sauce in a shallow skillet. Carefully break the eggs onto a small plate or saucer and slip them into the sauce without breaking the yolks. Simmer over low heat until the eggs are done.

Place two warm tortillas on each plate and top with the eggs. Pour over the remaining sauce and sprinkle the grated cheese over all. Serve with extra warm tortillas if desired.

Note: A variation would be to poach or fry the eggs separately, place on a plate, pour over the warm chili sauce, and serve the tortillas on the side. The eggs could also be garnished with crumbled chorizo or avocado slices.

SCRAMBLED EGGS WITH CHILI

SERVES 4

 8 eggs
 1 teaspoon salt
12 green chilies, peeled,
   seeded and chopped
 2 tablespoons bacon fat
   or cooking oil

Beat the eggs slightly until the yolks and whites are broken but not well mixed. Season with the salt and add the chilies.

Heat the fat until hot but not smoking. Add the egg mixture and reduce the heat, cooking slowly and stirring occasionally until the eggs are firm. Serve with bacon, ham, or sausage.

Note: For a heartier dish, add some tomatoes, peeled and chopped, onions, cubed or grated cheese, parsley or even fried tortillas cut into 8 or 10 sections.

EGGS WITH CHORIZO

1 cup sliced chorizo
1 tablespoon bacon fat
    or oil
8 eggs, slightly beaten
    Salt and pepper
4 tablespoons chopped
    chives
    Warm tortillas

Heat the fat and brown the chorizo. Add the eggs and season with salt and pepper to taste. Divide the egg-chorizo mixture when done and top with the chives. Serve with warm tortillas.

Note: If chorizo is purchased commercially, remove from the casing before cooking. The chives in this recipe can be replaced with onion, which should be sautéed along with the chorizo. A cup of green or red chili sauce can also be added along with the beaten eggs.

POACHED EGGS WITH CHILI

1 tablespoon fat or
    cooking oil
1 tablespoon all-purpose
    flour
½ teaspoon salt
½ teaspoon chili powder,
    or to taste
½ cup water
6 eggs
    Warm tortillas

Melt the fat in a heavy skillet and blend in the flour and salt. Add the chili powder to the desired pungency. Stir in the water and cook over medium heat until the mixture begins to thicken. Break the eggs onto a small plate or saucer and slip them into the sauce without breaking the yolks. Simmer until the eggs are firm. Serve hot with warm tortillas.

SOUPS

Mountainous New Mexico is not all that arid desert many people think it is. In fact, the Land of Enchantment is ski country—some of the best in the Rockies—and hearty soups are a part of its basic cookery.

Potatoes, beans, tomatoes, and chili are incorporated in any variety of ways, as well as the avocado, served hot in the winter and delightfully chilled in the summer.

PINTO BEAN SOUP

SERVES 8

2 cups pinto beans
2 quarts water
1 clove garlic, peeled
1 large onion, chopped
1 tablespoon dried
  oregano
2 teaspoons salt
2 red chili pods, stems
  and seeds removed

Soak the beans overnight, drain and then cook slowly in the water. After an hour, add all the other ingredients and simmer until the beans are tender. Pass the mixture through a colander using the liquid left over from the beans and enough water to make a soup of desired consistency. Reheat and serve hot. Tomatoes can also be added with excellent results.

CHILI POTATO SOUP

SERVES 6

4 large potatoes, diced
1 large onion, chopped
½ cup chopped celery
2 tablespoons bacon fat
  or oil
1 cup chopped green
  chilies
1 teaspoon salt
1 quart milk

Cook the potatoes in salted water until done.

Sauté the onion and celery in the hot fat. Stir in the potatoes and mix well. Add the chilies, salt, and milk and bring to a slow boil. Serve immediately.

Note: Grated cheese can be sprinkled on top if desired.

TORTILLA SOUP

6 corn tortillas
1 onion, chopped
1 clove garlic, minced
2 red chili pods, stems and seeds removed
2 tablespoons olive oil
3 cups chicken broth
1 1-pound can tomatoes with liquid
1 teaspoon salt
¼ teaspoon pepper
1 teaspoon chili powder
½ cup grated Cheddar cheese

Cut the tortillas into ½-inch strips and set aside.

Sauté the onion, garlic, and chilies in the hot oil until tender. Add all the other ingredients except the tortillas and cheese and simmer for about 30 minutes. Add the tortillas and continue simmering for another 30 minutes. Sprinkle the cheese on top and serve.

CORN SOUP

1 medium onion, chopped
2 tablespoons cooking oil
1 medium can tomatoes, peeled and chopped
2 quarts chicken stock
2 teaspoons salt
Pepper to taste
4 large ears corn
½ pound Cheddar cheese, cut into strips
1 tablespoon chopped parsley

Sauté the onion in the hot oil until tender. Add the tomatoes and simmer for 5 minutes. Add the chicken stock and bring to a boil. Season with the salt and pepper to taste.

Cut the kernels from the cobs and add to the soup mixture. Simmer for 10 minutes. Strain the pulp and put in a blender with a little of the liquid. Blend until liquefied and return to the broth. Bring the soup to a boil and add the cheese and parsley.

AVOCADO SOUP

2 tablespoons minced
   onion
1 tablespoon butter
1 tablespoon all-purpose
   flour
2 cups chicken stock
1 tomato peeled,
   seeded, and
   chopped
2 cups heavy cream
   or sour cream
1 teaspoon salt
   Pepper to taste
3 ripe avocados, peeled
2 teaspoons lemon juice

Sauté the onion slightly in the butter and stir in the flour to make a paste. Stir in the broth a little at a time, reserving some to purée with the avocados and lemon juice. Add the tomato, cream, salt and pepper to the soup mixture. Purée the avocados with the lemon juice. Combine both mixtures and chill thoroughly. Serve with fried tortilla squares, garlic toast or French bread.

SANDWICHES

Tacos, of course, are the sandwiches of Santa Fe cookery. But chopped or sliced chili, leftover pinto beans, and avocados can be used in different combinations with other ingredients to make some tasty sandwiches.

Hamburgers, for instance, take on a new dimension when served with cold chili sauce (salsa) of chopped chilies, tomatoes, onion, garlic, and salt.

Pinto beans can be refried with salt cracklings, onion, or garlic, spread on warm flour or corn tortillas, folded and served a dozen to the plate can be a delight to little hands.

Beans can also be mixed with chili sauce, or they can be added to chopped nuts and salad dressing, and served with lettuce between two slices of bread.

PINTO BEAN SANDWICH   *MAKES 4*

1 cup cooked drained
   pinto beans
1 small onion, chopped
½ cup chopped green
   chilies
1 dill pickle, minced
2 tablespoons ketchup
2 tablespoons
   prepared mustard
1 teaspoon salt
   Pepper to taste
8 slices bread
   Lettuce

Mash the pinto beans and mix well with the onion, chilies, and pickle. Season with the ketchup, mustard, salt, and pepper to taste. Blend together, spread on the bread, and top with the lettuce.

Note: Other ingredients can be added or substituted such as chopped egg, green pepper, raisins, nuts, garlic, and celery.

CHILI HAMBURGERS   *MAKES 12*

1 pound lean ground
   beef
1 onion, chopped
2 cups cooked pinto
   beans
½ cup chopped green
   chilies
1 8-ounce can
   tomatoes, drained
1 teaspoon salt
12 hamburger rolls,
   toasted
1 cup grated Cheddar
   cheese

Brown the beef and onion. Add the pinto beans, chilies, tomatoes, and salt. Divide on toasted buns and sprinkle with the cheese.

AVOCADO AND BACON SANDWICH

MAKES 4

2 tablespoons mayonnaise
1 teaspoon lemon juice
8 slices bread, toasted
1 ripe avocado, peeled and sliced
Salt and pepper to taste
½ pound bacon, fried

Mix the mayonnaise with the lemon juice and spread on the 4 slices of the toast. Lay the avocado slices which have been seasoned with the salt and pepper to taste and the bacon on the toast. Top with the other slices of toast.

AVOCADO AND CHILI SANDWICH

MAKES 4

2 ripe avocados, peeled and mashed
2 fresh green chilies, chopped
1 tablespoon lemon juice
Dash of Tabasco
½ small onion, chopped
1 tablespoon ketchup
1 teaspoon salt
8 slices bread

Mix all the ingredients and spread on the bread slices. Add lettuce leaves if desired.

CHEESE AND CHILI SANDWICH

MAKES 4

4 slices Swiss or American cheese
½ cup chopped green chilies
4 slices bread
Prepared mustard (optional)

Toast one side of the bread slices under the broiler. Put the slices of cheese and chilies on the un-toasted side and put back under the broiler until the cheese melts. Spread a little mustard on top, if desired.

CHILI CLUB SANDWICH

4 French sandwich rolls
2 cups refried pinto
    beans
4 slices boiled ham
4 slices cooked chicken
4 slices Swiss or
    American cheese
½ cup chopped green
    chilies
1 tomato, sliced
1 avocado, peeled and
    sliced
    Lettuce leaves
    Mustard

Slice the rolls lengthwise and remove part of the center. Put some of the beans on one half of each roll, then top with ham, chicken, cheese, chilies, tomato, avocado, and lettuce. Spread some mayonnaise on the other half of the rolls.

BREADS

The tortilla, as pointed out in the opening chapter, is the bread of Santa Fe cookery because it is used in the creation of so many dishes, such as tacos, enchiladas, tostadas, and burritos.

But there are other breads that are just as much a part of Santa Fe cookery, specifically sopaipillas, Indian bread, and buñuelos.

Sopaipillas are puffy, hollow crusts of deep-fried bread which are a must topped with honey alongside a combination plate. A sopaipilla mix is available commercially, but they are not that difficult to make from scratch.

Buñuelos are similar to sopaipillas and can be served either as a bread or dessert with a cinnamon-sugar coating or a glaze. They are a traditional Christmas treat.

Sweet rolls (molletes) are another favorite and often served with coffee or chocolate.

SOPAIPILLAS

4 cups all-purpose
    flour
1 teaspoon salt
2 teaspoons sugar
1 tablespoon baking
    powder
3 tablespoons lard or
    vegetable shortening
¾ cup warm water
    Cooking oil

Sift the flour with the salt, sugar, and baking powder and cut in the lard. Add enough of the warm water to make a smooth, dry dough. Cover and let stand for 30 minutes.

Roll out on a lightly floured board to ¼ inch thick. Cut into 3-inch squares and fry in the hot oil until golden brown on both sides, turning once. Drain and serve warm with honey.

Note: Sopaipillas can also be stuffed with any combination of refried beans, browned ground beef, onion and cheese. A slit is made on one side of each sopaipilla, allowing one to two per person, stuffed and baked at 350 degrees until the grated cheese is melted. They should be served with a green or red chili sauce.

SANTA FE CORN BREAD

1 large can creamed-
    style corn
2 eggs, slightly beaten
¾ cup milk
¼ cup salad oil
1 cup yellow cornmeal
1 cup chopped green
    chilies
1 teaspoon baking
    powder
1 teaspoon salt
2 cups grated Cheddar
    cheese

Combine all the ingredients and put in a lightly greased 9x9x2-inch pan. Bake, uncovered, at 400 degrees for about 45 minutes, or until firm.

BUÑUELOS

4 cups all-purpose
   flour, sifted
1 teaspoon salt
4 teaspoons baking
   powder
2 tablespoons lard
1½ cups warm water
   Cooking oil

Sift the flour with the salt and baking powder. Cut in the lard and add the water to make a smooth dough. Divide into 12 to 15 balls. Let stand for 20 minutes.

Roll out each ball on a lightly-floured board until about 5 inches in diameter.

Deep fry in the hot oil until brown, about 30 seconds on each side. Drain. Sprinkle with honey, sugar or a cinnamon-sugar mixture made by combining 1 cup sugar and 1 teaspoon ground cinnamon in a paper bag. Coat the buñuelos one at a time in the bag as one would to dredge chicken pieces.

RED CHILI
BUTTERMILK BISCUITS

2 cups all-purpose flour
½ teaspoon salt
2½ teaspoons baking
   powder
½ teaspoon baking soda
1 tablespoon red chili
   powder
⅓ cup butter, softened
¾ cup buttermilk
2 tablespoons melted
   butter

Sift the flour together with the salt, baking powder, and baking soda. Stir in the chili powder. Add the butter and blend well. Stir in the buttermilk until the dough is soft. Knead on a lightly floured board for a few minutes and then roll out to ½ inch thick.

Cut into 2-inch pieces. Place on a greased baking sheet and brush tops with the melted butter. Bake at 450 degrees for about 15 minutes.

INDIAN BREAD

1 package active dry
    yeast
½ cup lukewarm water
2 teaspoons salt
1 teaspoon sugar
2 tablespoons melted
    shortening
1½ cups hot water
5 cups all-purpose flour

Stir the yeast into the warm water and dissolve. Blend the salt, sugar, and shortening with the hot water in a large bowl. Beat in 1 cup of flour and then add the yeast mixture. Mix well. Then add 3 more cups of the flour, reserving the last one for kneading.

Turn the dough out onto a floured kneading board or other smooth surface and knead for 10 minutes, or until smooth and elastic, adding additional flour as necessary to keep the dough from sticking to the board.

Cover and let rise in a warm place until doubled in bulk. Punch down and repeat process twice more until it has risen three times in all.

Shape into 2 round loaves and put on 9-inch pie plates. Brush with a little more melted shortening. Cover and let stand another 30 minutes.

Bake at 350 degrees for 45 to 60 minutes. For a crisper crust, place a pan of water in the oven but not below the loaves.

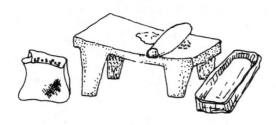

100

2 cups milk
2 packages active dry yeast
¼ cup honey
4 cups unbleached white flour
4 cups whole wheat flour
2 cups cooked pinto beans, mashed
2 teaspoons salt
2 tablespoons shortening

Scald the milk and allow to cool to lukewarm.

Dissolve the yeast in the milk and then add the honey and half of the flour, 2 cups of each. Mix well, cover, and let stand in a warm place until light and spongy.

Blend in all the remaining ingredients except 1 cup of the white flour.

Turn out on a floured board. Using the last cup of flour, knead for 10 minutes, or until the dough is smooth and elastic.

Cover and let rise in a warm place until double in bulk, about 1 hour.

Punch down, cover with a damp towel, and let stand for 10 minutes.

Shape into three or four loaves and place in greased pans. Cover the pans and let the dough rise until the loaves do not spring back when pressed, about 45 minutes.

Bake at 350 degrees for 50 minutes, or until nicely browned. Cool on racks.

(Molletes)
SWEET ROLLS

2 packages active dry yeast
1½ cups plus 2 teaspoons sugar
2 cups lukewarm water
6 cups all-purpose flour
½ cup shortening
2 eggs, slightly beaten
1 teaspoon salt
1 teaspoon aniseed
3 tablespoons melted butter

Dissolve the yeast with 2 tablespoons sugar in the lukewarm water. Sift the flour and combine 3 cups with the yeast mixture. Let stand in a warm place for 2 hours.

Cream the shortening with the 1½ cups sugar and add to the yeast flour mixture. Combine the eggs, salt, aniseed, with the other 3 cups of flour and blend well.

Knead on a lightly floured board until smooth and elastic. Place in a greased bowl, turn to coat other side of dough, cover with a damp towel and allow to double in bulk in a warm place.

Punch down and knead. Allow to double in bulk again, about 45 minutes.

Mold the dough into small muffins about the size of medium eggs. Place in greased tins, cover and let rise until double in bulk, about 1 hour.

Brush with the melted butter. Bake at 350 degrees for about 30 minutes, or until done. Regular dinner rolls can be made from the same recipe by eliminating the eggs, 1½ cups sugar, and the aniseed.

PIÑON NUTS

The piñon nut is indigenous to the southern Rocky Mountains and has found a home in Santa Fe cookery. The piñon pines which produce the very edible nut are usually smaller than other varieties of pine trees and are found at elevations of 4,000 to about 7,500 feet.

The tiny seeds can be eaten raw, roasted, or in cookies, soups, pies, biscuits, and anything else the innovative cook can come up with. They are rich in protein and fat, having more than 3,000 calories to the pound.

Early-arriving Spaniards found the Indians harvesting them and Coronado made mention of them in 1540. The Navajos made it a major industry in trading with other tribes, and even today they still collect them for commercial purposes.

Piñon nuts are seeds enclosed in cones. In September, usually after the first frost, the mature cones open and the nuts fall. The oldest and most simple method of harvesting the nuts is to gather them off the ground by hand. A fast picker, working a plentiful crop, can pick 20 pounds of nuts in a day.

Piñons lose 7 to 15 percent of their moisture within 30 days after being harvested To properly cure the nuts, dry air is required. The nuts should be stored in cloth bags with ventilation between the bags.

A most favorable characteristic of piñons is their excellent keeping qualities. Dry, unshelled nuts have been marketed with good results after 3 years of storage in New Mexico's dry air.

Shelled nuts become rancid after 3 to 6 months. Unshelled nuts are sometimes roasted, and, while this improves their flavor, they should not be stored in this form for too long as they may become rancid more quickly.

The piñon nut apparently does not become rancid so long as the germ retains its vitality. The vitality is greatly prolonged if humidity is kept below 60 percent or as low as 40 during warmer periods.

The tannin in the shell and in the seed coat of the kernel may function in preserving the fat and oil of the nuts. Oxidative changes in the oil or fat cause rancidity.

The protein average for piñon nuts is 14.5 percent, higher than that of pecans (10.4), and about the same as English walnuts and Brazil nuts.

The piñon nut kernels average about 60 percent oil or fat. This is lower than pecans, English walnuts, and Brazil nuts. The carbohydrate content averages 18.8 percent.

The piñons can be roasted in the oven at 300 degrees by placing the unshelled nuts in a shallow pan, stirring them frequently, and testing them occasionally to make sure they are not overdone. Another method used is to cook them in a heavy skillet on top of the stove, again stirring frequently. It is very easy to overcook piñons.

For a salt flavor, the nuts can be washed in salt water or dampened and sprinkled with salt as they roast.

Piñons are available by mail from several outlets in New Mexico (see Outlets and Specialty Stores).

PIÑON NUT COOKIES

MAKES 2 DOZEN

½ cup butter, softened
½ cup shortening
½ teaspoon vanilla
　　extract
1 cup flour, sifted
½ cup sugar
½ teaspoon ground
　　cinnamon
¾ cup piñon nuts,
　　shelled

Cream the butter, shortening, and vanilla together. Mix the flour with the sugar and cinnamon and add along with the nuts to the butter mixture. Blend well.

Drop by spoonfuls onto an ungreased baking sheet. Bake at 425 degrees for about 10 minutes, or until light brown.

PIÑON NUT MUFFINS

MAKES 1 DOZEN

6 ounces warm milk
6 tablespoons honey
1 cup piñon nuts, shelled
1½ cups flour
1 teaspoon salt
1 tablespoon baking
　　powder

Mix the milk, honey, and piñon nuts. Sift the flour, salt, and baking powder together. Combine and pour into greased muffin tins, filling only halfway.

Bake at 425 degrees for 30 minutes, or until nicely browned.

PIÑON NUT PIE

MAKES 1 9-INCH PIE

1 9-inch pie crust
4 tablespoons butter,
　　softened
1 cup dark brown sugar
3 eggs
1 cup heavy cream
½ teaspoon salt
1½ cups piñon nuts,
　　shelled
1 teaspoon vanilla
　　extract

Prepare the pie crust as directed.

Cream the butter with the sugar and beat in the eggs. Mix in the remaining ingredients, reserving some of the nuts to sprinkle on top.

Spoon mixture into pie crust, top with the nuts and bake at 450 degrees for 15 minutes. Reduce the oven temperature to 325 degrees and bake for another 20 minutes, or until done.

PIÑON NUT CANDY

1 cup granulated sugar
1 cup firmly packed
    dark brown sugar
½ cup water
1 stick butter
1 tablespoon white
    vinegar
1 cup piñon nuts, shelled

Mix the sugars, water, butter, and vinegar in a saucepan. Bring to a boil and heat until 234 degrees to 240 degrees. Cool and beat in the nuts. Drop by spoonfuls onto a buttered pan or oiled paper.

DESSERTS,
CHEESE, AND BEVERAGES

After a swing along the rainbow of Santa Fe cookery, the pot of gold is, of course, at the end—light and tasty desserts. They are for example: flan (custard), puddings, biscochitos (aniseed cookies), fruit turnovers (see Empanadas), buñuelos (see Breads), and cake.

Perhaps, to top off a fine dining experience, there's native goat's cheese and such beverages as hot chocolate and atole (gruel drink).

FLAN

1½ cups sugar.
1 cup water
3 cups milk
1 teaspoon vanilla
   extract
½ teaspoon ground
   cinnamon
¼ teaspoon salt
6 eggs, slightly beaten
   Crushed nuts (optional)

Caramelize the 1¼ cups sugar with the water over low heat in a small skillet. Place the caramel mixture in the bottom of six custard cups. Set aside and cool.

In a double boiler, combine the milk, vanilla, cinnamon, salt, and the ¼ cup sugar and bring to a gentle boil. Cool and then combine with the eggs (some cooks prefer to separate the eggs before beating).

Pour the flan into the six cups and place these in a large pan containing hot water. Bake at 350 degrees for about 1 hour, or until a knife inserted in the flan comes out clean. Serve either hot or cold, and sprinkled with crushed nuts, if desired.

(Sprouted Wheat Pudding)
PANOCHA

4 cups (1 pound)
   panocha flour
2 cups all-purpose flour,
   sifted
½ teaspoon salt
6 cups boiling water
1 cup dark brown sugar
   (instead of sugar, 2
   large cones of pilon-
   cillo, unrefined
   brown sugar)

Combine the flours and salt and add the boiling water. Mix until smooth. Cover and let stand for 15 minutes. Add the sugar or pilon-cillo, finely shaved. When completely mixed, put the mixture in a greased oven-proof pot and boil for 30 minutes. Cover and bake at 350 degrees for 1½ to 2 hours, or until thick and dark brown.

SOPA (Bread Pudding)

1 loaf white or Indian
    bread, sliced
1 cup granulated sugar
1 cup dark brown sugar
4 cups hot water
1 tablespoon ground
    cinnamon
1 teaspoon vanilla
    extract
1 tablespoon butter
1 cup raisins
1 pound Longhorn
    cheese, sliced

Lightly toast the bread until dry.

Caramelize the sugars in a large skillet, stirring constantly. Slowly add the water. Then add the cinnamon, vanilla, and butter. Boil for 5 to 10 minutes, or until thick.

Layer a large casserole with slices of toast. Add the raisins and cheese. Repeat until all the ingredients are used up. Pour the hot syrup over casserole.

Bake at 300 degrees for about 30 minutes, or until the cheese is well melted.

RICE PUDDING

2 cups water
1 cup rice
1 teaspoon salt
1 cinnamon stick
1 piece lemon peel
    (optional)
1 cup sugar
4 cups milk
2 egg yolks, lightly
    beated

Bring the water to a boil and add the rice, salt, cinnamon stick, and lemon peel. Simmer until the water is absorbed. Discard the cinnamon stick and lemon peel. Add the sugar and milk and continue boiling until the pudding is thick and the rice is soft. Remove from the heat and stir in the egg yolks until the mixture has the consistency of a custard.

Bring to a boil and simmer for about 5 minutes, stirring constantly. Pour into individual cups or a 6½-cup ring mold and chill thoroughly. The pudding can be topped with whipped cream, nuts, or ground cinnamon if desired.

(Aniseed Cookies)
BISCOCHITOS

MAKES 4 DOZEN

2 cups lard
1¼ cups sugar
2 teaspoons aniseed
2 egg yolks, slightly beaten
6 cups all-purpose flour
3 tablespoons baking powder
1 teaspoon salt
½ cup water
1 teaspoon ground cinnamon

Cream the lard with the 1 cup sugar and the aniseed. Add the egg yolks.

Sift together the flour, baking powder, and salt. Mix in the water.

Combine the two mixtures and knead until well mixed. Roll out to a ¼-inch thickness and cut into fancy shapes.

Combine the remaining ¼ cup sugar and cinnamon and dust the top of the cookies. Bake at 350 degrees for 8 to 10 minutes, or until lightly browned.

CINNAMON PEACHES

SERVES 4

1 can peach halves
1 lemon
2 tablespoons melted butter or margarine
¼ cup sugar
2 teaspoons ground cinnamon

Drain the peaches. Sprinkle with lemon juice and then brush with butter. Sprinkle with sugar, more lemon juice, and cinnamon. Place the peaches on a baking sheet or pan and broil until golden brown.

PINTO BEAN CAKE

2 cups all-purpose flour
1 teaspoon baking powder
½ teaspoon baking soda
½ teaspoon salt
½ cup butter, softened
1 cup sugar
2 eggs, beaten
1 cup warm water
1 cup cooked pinto beans, mashed
1 cup diced apples
1 cup raisins
1 cup chopped nuts
1 teaspoon vanilla extract

Sift together the flour, baking powder, baking soda, and salt.

Cream the butter, sugar, and eggs together. Add the water and flour mixture alternately. Stir in the pinto beans, apples, raisins, nuts and vanilla.

Bake in a greased round or square pan or two small loaf pans at 350 degrees for about 45 minutes. When cool, cover with a frosting, if desired.

NATIVE GOAT'S CHEESE

1 rennet tablet
4 teaspoons water
1 gallon fresh goat's milk or whole milk

Crush and dissolve the tablet in the water. Warm the milk to 90 degrees and add the tablet. When a firm clabber forms, about 30 minutes, pour the mixture into a cheesecloth bag. Hang the curd up to drain away the whey. After the water has drained for a few hours, form the curds into a block, squeezing out the last bits of moisture through the cheesecloth. Serve plain or with guava jelly, piñon nuts, sesame seeds, syrup, or fruit.

GREEN (RED) CHILI JELLY

MAKES 4 JARS

4 fresh green chilies (or canned) or 4 dried red chili pods
4 sweet green or red peppers
1 cup white vinegar
5½ cups sugar
1 bottle pectin (Certo) or one box Sure-Jell

Roast and peel the green chilies, remove stems and seeds. Or wash the red chili pods and remove stems and seeds. Grind the peppers, both sweet and hot, in a food processor, chopper, or blender. Add the vinegar and sugar. Boil until the mixture is transparent. Cool for 5 minutes and add the pectin. Stir thoroughly and skim off any foam. Pour into jars and seal.

ATOLE (Gruel)

SERVES 6 TO 8

1 cup blue cornmeal
½ teaspoon salt
2 cups water
2 cups milk
Sugar to taste

Mix the cornmeal, salt, and water together. Boil until the mixture is thick. Add the milk and sugar to taste and simmer, stirring constantly, until thickened. Serve hot with additional sugar, if desired.

(Hot Corn Drink)
PINOLE

MAKES 1½ CUPS

1 cup blue or white cornmeal
¼ cup sugar
¼ teaspoon ground cinnamon
Fresh milk, hot

Brown the cornmeal in a 425-degree oven, stirring occasionally, about 10 minutes. Add the sugar and cinnamon. Use as cocoa in hot milk.

SERVES 6

HOT CHOCOLATE

4 ounces Mexican
   chocolate (cocoa or
   sweet)
4 cups milk
1 teaspoon ground
   cinnamon
¼ cup sugar
1 tablespoon vanilla
   extract
⅛ teaspoon salt

Combine all the ingredients in a saucepan or double boiler and cook over a low heat, stirring constantly to prevent scorching, until the chocolate is melted. Beat until frothy and serve hot in cups.

SERVES 4

CAFÉ CON LECHE

2 cups hot milk
2 cups hot coffee,
   triple strength

Fill coffee cups half full (or less according to taste) with the hot milk. Add the hot coffee and serve hot.

SERVES 1

MARGARITA

1 slice of lime or lemon
1 tablespoon of salt
1½ ounces white tequila
1½ ounces Triple Sec
1 ounce fresh lime or
   lemon juice
   Crushed ice

Chill a large cocktail glass. Rub the rim with a slice of lime and dip into plate of salt.

Mix tequila, Triple Sec, lime juice, and ice cubes. Pour the mixture through a strainer into the prepared glass. Garnish with a slice of fresh lime or lemon.

TYPICAL MENUS

BREAKFAST

Fresh Orange Juice with Frosted Raspberries
Green Chili Omelette with Snappy Cheese
and lots of Fresh Tomatoes, chopped
French Fries
Café con Leche

Well-seasoned Tomato Juice
Huevos Rancheros in Chafing Dish
Bacon Strips
Warm Tortillas
Chilled Milk

Fresh Grapefruit with Cherry Centers
Eggs Scrambled with Salsa
Homemade Chorizo
English Muffins, Toasted, Buttered and
Spread with a Tart Marmalade
Coffee

Cinnamon Peaches
Hot Biscuits and Sweet Rolls
Dressed with Red Chili Jelly
Hot Chocolate

Grapefruit Juice
Poached Eggs with Chili and Salsa
Hot Buñuelos with Honey and Butter
Atole

LUNCH

Hardy Pinto Bean Soup
Tacos, about three
Creamy Flan
Clusters of Raisins and Cinnamon Pecans
Iced Tea

Chilled Avocado Soup
Grilled Cheese and Chili Sandwiches
Pinto Bean Salad
Rice Pudding
Coffee

A Super Combination Plate:
Taco, Enchilada, Pinto Beans Sprinkled
with Cheese, a side of
Mexican Rice
Hot Sopaipillas with Honey and Butter
Scoops of Pineapple Sherbert
Café con Leche

Hot Corn Soup
Avocado and Bacon Sandwiches
Chili Coleslaw
Assorted Cheeses With
Slices of Apples
Milk

Halved Cantaloupes
Hot Potato Salad
Santa Fe Corn Bread
Pinto Bean Cake
Pinole

Chili con Carne
Stacks of Warm Tortillas
Avocado and Tomato Salad
Panocha Pudding
Hot Chocolate

DINNER

Arroz con Pollo
Green Chili and Squash Casserole
Sliced Pinto Bean Bread
Flan and Assorted Cookies
Atole

Enchiladas, about three
Pinto Bean and Carrot Casserole
Chili Cottage Cheese Salad
Piñon Nut Cookies
Hot Chocolate

Tortilla Soup
Platter of Chili Rellenos
With a side of Chicos
Refried Pinto Beans
Red Chili Buttermilk Biscuits
Rice Pudding sprinkled with Cinnamon
Café con Leche

Carne Adovada
Baked Corn
Mexican Rice
Guacamole Salad
Tortillas or Crispy Chips
Sopa (Bread Pudding)
Pinole

Slices of Pinto Bean Loaf
Eggplant and Chili Casserole
Indian Bread
Orange and Avocado Salad
Glazed Buñuelos
Coffee

Chilled Avocado Soup
Green Chili Casserole
Pinto Beans and Rice
Sopaipillas and Honey
Piñon Nut Pie
Milk

HOLIDAY DINNER BUFFET

Assorted Dips with Plenty of Chips:
Chili con Queso, Guacamole Dip, Pinto Bean Dip
Miniature Tacos, Pickled Jalapeños
Rolled Enchiladas, Tamales, Chalupas,
Pinto Beans and Posole Stew served in large pots
Warm Tortillas Stacked
Avocado Salad
Fruit Empanadas
Café con Leche
Hot Chocolate

ALTITUDE COOKING

At high altitudes, as in Santa Fe, the cook must rise to the occasion. Adjustments have to be made in baking, boiling water, pressure cooking, making candy, cooking vegetables, deep-fat frying, canning.

Sea level recipes should be adjusted at 7,000 feet (Santa Fe) with one of the following changes when applicable. For every 1 teaspoon of baking powder called for, use only ¾ teaspoon. Decrease to ½ teaspoon of baking soda for every cup of sour liquid. Add an extra large egg, and do not beat eggs. For every cup called for, save 2 tablespoons of sugar. Increase the liquid 3 tablespoons for every cup indicated. Add 1 tablespoon additional flour. Decrease the amount of butter by a couple of tablespoons in a rich recipe and turn up the oven 25 degrees.

In the higher, thinner atmosphere, there is, naturally, more carbon dioxide in the air,which expands quicker and therefore produces a greater leavening action.

The higher the altitude, the lower the boiling point, as follows:

Sea Level	212°F.
2,000 feet	208°
5,000 feet	202°
7,000 feet	198°
10,000 feet	194°
15,000 feet	185°

In any cooking involving moisture, such as vegetables, more liquid and more time will be required than at sea level. Frozen whole beets and carrots, for instance, will take many more minutes to cook at, say, 7,000 feet, while shredded vegetables will take only a short time longer.

Candy, then, should be cooked to a lower temperature to allow for faster evaporation. Generally speaking, allow one degree less for every 500 feet, as according to this comparative chart:

	Sea Level	5,000 Feet	7,000 Feet
Soft Ball	234°-240°F.	224°-230°F.	219°-225°F.
Firm Ball	242°-248°	232°-238°	227°-233°
Hard Ball	250°-268°	240°-258°	235°-253°
Soft Crack	270°-290°	260°-280°	255°-275°
Hard Crack	300°-310°	290°-300°	285°-295°

The rule for pressure cooking is to maintain the same amount of cooking time as at sea level but to allow a ½-pound increase for every 1,000 feet.

Canning in a boiling water bath requires a 1-minute increase in the processing time for every 1,000 feet above sea level if the cooking time is 20 minutes or less and 2 minutes for every 1,000 feet if the processing time is more than 20 minutes.

Deep-fat frying, as in boiling water, will necessitate a lower temperature, about 10 degrees lower at 5,000 feet and 15 degrees at 7,000 feet.

Roasts are not affected much by altitudes up to 7,000 feet, but they do require a longer cooking time above sea level.

Because of the evaporation, pies need a bit more water than at sea level, while with cookies, as with cakes, it is best to reduce the amount of baking powder, soda, and sugar above 5,000 feet.

Bread dough takes a shorter time to rise at higher

altitudes and quick breads require a hotter oven and less baking powder. For example use ¾ teaspoon for 1 teaspoon at 5,000 feet and ½ teaspoon at 7,000 feet and above.

Jelly and preserves should be cooked 7 degrees above the boiling point as shown in the chart for water, i.e., 209 degrees at 5,000 feet and 205 degrees at 7,000 feet.

QUESTIONS and ANSWERS

WHAT IS THE DIFFERENCE BETWEEN RED AND GREEN CHILI? WHICH IS HOTTER?

Chili is green before it turns red; it can be picked and eaten in both stages with the red chili being dried in the sun for use year round. As to the "hotness," it all depends on the variety purchased. A talk with your retail seller will usually set you straight.

WHAT TYPE OF CHEESE IS USED AS A RULE?

Sharp cheddar is preferred by restaurants but mild cheddar or a mild domestic Muenster can be used. Californians prefer Monterey Jack.

ARE CANNED CHILIS O.K.?

Yes, as long as the green chili is not canned in oil. Look for "whole green chilies, roasted & peeled" on the label.

WHAT IS "BLUE CORNMEAL"?

Blue corn is grown in New Mexico and is used by both Indian and Hispanic cooks. The corn is really blue in color, sometimes so blue it is almost black.

HOW HOT IS HOT WITH CHILI?

Who's to say? What may be hot to me could be mild to the next person and vice versa.

WHAT IS THE BEST WAY TO TAKE AWAY THE BURN WHILE EATING CHILI?

A glass of water will not do it, beer is better, or tea, coffee and milk.

IS WINE RECOMMENDED?

I think a dry white wine is very good with hot chili; reds seem to be a little heavy and a sweet wine would never do. Sangria is also very good with spicy food.

WHAT IS THE DIFFERENCE BETWEEN FLOUR TORTILLAS AND CORN TORTILLAS?

A flour tortilla is thicker and more like a grilled bread. The corn tortilla does not rise.

WHICH SAUCE SHOULD I USE?

After experiencing New Mexican dishes you will soon have your favorite sauces. There are not hard and fast rules.

WHY IS A FRIED EGG ON TOP OF SOME ENCHILADAS?

It seems to be a recent innovation created by the Anglo influence. The egg helps to take the burn out of the chili.

HOW DO YOU PREVENT AVOCADO FROM TURNING IN COLOR?

Squeeze a few drops of fresh lemon juice on it.

IS CHILI A PEPPER?

Chili is the Aztec name for the plant Capsicum frutescens. Columbus found chili in the West Indies in 1493 and because of the pungency of the pods he called the plant pepper.

IS JALAPEÑO REALLY THE HOTTEST CHILI?

Chili Cayenne is hotter; you must be very careful to remove the seeds and veins as they will modify it somewhat.

DOES EVERYTHING HAVE TO BE MADE FROM SCRATCH?

No, there are many mixes for sopaipillas, canned sauces, canned chilis, canned and frozen tortillas, etc., in the markets.

CAN I COOK NEW MEXICAN FOOD FOR ONE OR TWO PEOPLE?

It would be difficult but you can always freeze the leftover sauce and tortillas and have them ready for another meal.

HOW LONG WILL LEFTOVERS KEEP?

The rules for any sauce, meat and bread should be followed in refrigeration storage or freezer.

HOW DOES ONE "DRESS UP" NEW MEXICAN FOOD?

It really isn't necessary; the red or green chili, yellow or white cheese, blue corn tortillas, tacos and enchiladas, all with generous servings of fresh lettuce and tomato, seem colorful enough for the eye.

CAN NEW MEXICAN FOOD BE CONSIDERED GOURMET?

Yes, if one is a connoisseur in the preparation and subtleties of the spices used in each dish.

WHAT KIND OF COOKWARE DO YOU RECOMMEND?

You probably have everything necessary for the preparation of these recipes in your kitchen. A good heavy griddle is used for tortillas, a large bean pot for frijoles and regular sauce pans. The casserole dishes are very nice when done in Mexican pottery and served in the same dish.

OUTLETS
AND SPECIALTY STORES

These outlets and stores carry various items used in recipes of *SANTA FE COOKERY*. A list of items may be obtained by writing to the addresses given.

ELENA'S KITCHEN
P.O. Box 2322
Santa Fe, NM 87501

CASADOS FARMS
P.O. Box 852
San Juan Pueblo, NM 87566

SEÑOR MURPHY, CANDYMAKER
127½ W. San Francisco St.
Santa Fe, NM 87501

BOLNER'S FIESTA PRODUCTS
426 Menchaca
San Antonio, TX 78207

GEBHARDT MEXICAN FOODS CO.
San Antonio, TX 78207

OLD EL PASO
Anthony, TX 88021

JOSIE'S BEST MEXICAN FOODS
1731 2nd Street
Santa Fe, NM 87501

LOS CHILEROS
1201 Cerrillos Rd.
Santa Fe, NM 87501

SANTA FE TRAYS
Fran Hogan
Rt. 8, Box 216X
Santa Fe, NM 87501

GLOSSARY

ALBONDIGAS (ahl-BON-dee-gahs)—Meat balls of varying sizes usually served as an appetizer.

ARROZ CON POLLO (ah-RROS kon POY-yoh)—Classic chicken and rice dish.

ATOLE (ah-TOLL-leh)—A gruel-like drink made with blue cornmeal.

BEEF JERKY—Dried strips of beef.

BISCOCHITOS (bees-coh-CHEE-tohs)—Aniseed cookies.

BUÑUELOS (boo-nyoo-WEH-lohs)—Fritters which are traditionally Christmas treats usually served with a syrup or cinnamon-sugar coating.

BURRITOS (boo-RREE-tohs)—Made with flour tortillas, filled with pinto beans and/or meat mixture, and topped with a chili sauce.

CALABACITAS (kah-lah-bah-SEE-tahs)—Summer squash.

CALABAZA (kah-lab-BAH-sah)—Baked pumpkin.

CALDILLO (kahl-DEE-yoh)—Stew made of meat, onions and potatoes.

CARNE ADOVADA (KAHR-neh ah-doh-VAH-dah)—Strips of pork marinated in a chili sauce.

CHALUPAS (chah-LOO-pahs)—Tostadas shaped into little boats and filled with pinto beans, chicken, lettuce, tomatoes, etc.

CHICARRONES (chee-chah-RROHN-ehs)—Cracklings.

CHICOS (chee-kohs)—Dried corn kernels.

CHILAQUILLAS (chee-lah-KEE-lahs)—Stale tortillas fried crisp and combined with beef or eggs, onions, tomatoes, cheese, and chili sauce.

CHILI CARIBE (CHEE-leh kah-REEB-eh)—Red chili pods with water and seasoned.

CHILI COLORADO—Red chili powder.

CHILI CON QUESO (CHEE-leh kon KEH-soh)—Dip of melted cheese and chili served with tostados.

CHILI, GREEN—Harvested from late July until October; roasted and peeled, the basis for sauces, relishes, and dips.

CHILI, RED—Harvested before the first frost, Sept. 16-Oct. 7, dried for later use and crushed into powder. Green chili ripens into red pods.

CHILI RELLENOS (CHEE-leh reh-YEH-nohs)—Peeled and whole green chili stuffed with cheese and/or meat which is deep fried in a cornmeal batter.

CHORIZO (choh-REE-soh)—Seasoned sausage usually served at breakfast but also used as a filling for enchiladas, empanadas, etc.

CILANTRO (see-LAHN-troh)—Coriander.

COMINO (koh-MEE-noh)—Cumin.

EMPANADAS (ehm-pah-NAH-dahs)—Turnovers stuffed with left-over meat, chicken, or shrimp, vegetables,or fruit, served as an appetizer, dessert, or buffet item.

ENCHILADAS (ehn-chee-LAH-dahs)—White or blue cornmeal tortillas that are stacked, rolled, or folded with any combination of meat, cheese, onion, tomato, lettuce, avocado, sour cream, chili sauce, etc.

ENSALADA (ehn-sah-LAH-dah)—Salad.

FLAN (flahn)—Light custard served in caramelized cups.

GARBANZOS (gahr-BAHN-zohs)—Chickpeas.

GUACAMOLE (gwah-kah-MOH-leh)—Dip of mashed avocados and seasonings served with tostadas. Also used as a salad on lettuce or as a garnish on enchiladas, tacos, etc.

HUEVOS RANCHEROS (HUEH-vohs rahn-CHEH-rohs)—Fried or poached eggs usually served on warm tortillas with a chili sauce and various garnishes.

INDIAN BREAD—Oval loafs with a hard crust.

JALAPEÑOS (hal-lah-PEH-nyos)—Small, green hot peppers excellent pickled or in sauces.

JICAMA (HEE-kah-mah)—Root vegetable often eaten raw in salads with a flavor between that of a crisp apple and Chinese water chestnuts.

MASA (MAH-sah)—Corn-based dough used to make tortillas and tamales.

MASA HARINA (MAH-sah ah-REE-nah)—Commercial mix of corn treated with lime water and specially ground corn flour used to make tortillas.

MASA TRIGO (MAH-sah TREE-goh)—Commercial mix composed of blended flour, shortening, salt, and leavening used for tortillas and tamales.

MENUDO (meh-NOO-thoh)—Tripe.

MOLE (MOH-leh)—Mexican chocolate sauce.

MOLLETES (moh-LEH-tehs)—Sweet aniseed rolls.

MORSILLO (mohr-SEE-yoh)—Blood pudding with raisins and piñon nuts.

NACHOS (NAH-chohs)—Corn chips topped with cheese and jalapeño strips, broiled and served as an appetizer.

NIXTAMALINA (nis-tah-ma-LEE-nah)—Fine-grade Mexican corn flour used as masa.

PANOCHA (pah-NOH-chah)—Sprouted wheat flour used to make a pudding of the same name.

PILONCILLO (pee-lohn-SEE-yoh)—Unrefined brown sugar hardened into cone shapes.

PINOLE (pee-NOH-leh)—Cornmeal drink made with sugar and cinnamon.

POSOLE (poh-SOH-leh)—Stew made with chicos (or posole) and pork.

QUELITES (keh-LEE-tehs)—Spinach with pinto beans and chili.

QUESADILLAS (keh-sah-DEE-yahs)—Tortillas folded around cheese and chili relish and deep fried.

QUESO FRESCO (KEH-soh FREHS-koh)—Fresh native goat's cheese.

REFRIED BEANS—Pinto beans which are mashed and refried in oil.

SALSA (SAHL-sah)—Chili sauce, green or red.

SOPA (SOH-pah)—Bread pudding with raisins, cinnamon, and cheese.

SOPAIPILLAS (SOH-pah-PEE-yahs)—Puffy, deep-fried bread traditionally served with honey.

TACOS (TAH-kohs)—Fried, crisp tortillas which are folded and stuffed with meat, chicken, or pinto beans, lettuce, tomato, onion, etc., and topped with a taco or chili sauce.

TAMALES (tah-MAHL-lehs)—A mixture of pork and red chili enclosed in masa, wrapped in cornhusks and steamed.

TORTILLAS (torh-TEE-yahs)—Thin pancakes made from masa and slightly fried before using for tacos, enchiladas, tostadas, etc.

TOSTADAS (tohs-TAH-thahs)—Crisp tortillas served open-faced with any combination of meat, chicken, pinto beans, lettuce, tomato, onion, sour cream, avocado, etc.

TOSTADOS (tohs-TAH-thohs)—Crisp tortillas cut into wedges and used for dips, hash, and soups.

INDEX